A Cappella

This book was developed for

the University of Iowa Press by

the Center for American Places,

Santa Fe, New Mexico,

and Harrisonburg, Virginia

(www.americanplaces.org).

A Cappella

Mennonite Voices in Poetry

edited by Ann Hostetler

University of Iowa Press ψ Iowa City

C

University of Iowa Press, Iowa City 52242

Printed in the United States of America

Design by Richard Hendel

http://www.uiowa.edu/uiowapress

The publication of this book was generously supported
by the University of Iowa Foundation.

Printed on acid-free paper

Library of Congress Cataloging-in-Publication Data
A cappella: Mennonite voices in poetry / edited by Ann
Hostetler.
p.   cm.
Includes bibliographical references and index.
ISBN 0-87745-874-X (cloth), ISBN 0-87745-859-6 (pbk.)
1. American poetry—Mennonite authors.   2. Mennonites—
Poetry.   I. Hostetler, Ann Elizabeth.
PS591.M43C37 2003
811.008'092287—dc21   2003048417

03   04   05   06   07   C   5   4   3   2   1
03   04   05   06   07   P   5   4   3   2   1

For those who came before and
left traces of their journeys

It only takes one person plowing a row
to make a field, then others can follow
knowing they aren't the first or alone.
—Julia Kasdorf, from "Boustrophedon"

Contents

Acknowledgments

As a form of community in print, an anthology results from the creative collaboration of many people. First of all, I wish to thank the poets who agreed to share their work in this volume. I also wish to thank the many poets who submitted work that does not appear in this volume. Because there were so many submissions, it was impossible to print all of the fine poetry I received. However, it was heartening to learn about the great number of practicing writers and writing groups among Mennonites, and I hope that this is only the first of many more such gatherings of poets.

I wish to acknowledge the Cincinnati Mennonite Fellowship's biannual Mennonite Arts Weekend, where I was inspired to create this anthology after learning of the variety of Mennonite poets and meeting several of the poets in this volume. George Thompson and Randall Jones of the Center for American Places provided a sustained vote of confidence in the project and suggestions for the shaping of the manuscript. Ervin Beck, Todd Davis, Julia Kasdorf, John D. Roth, Beth Martin Birky, and Hildi Froese Tiessen read versions of the manuscript and offered invaluable suggestions. Ervin Beck provided essential bibliographical information, without which this volume would have been far less complete. Joe Springer, curator of the Mennonite Historical Library at Goshen College, provided copies of rare books and biographical resources. I am grateful to Ross Bay, Annabeth Keim, Krista Lehman, Rebecca Rich, and Elizabeth Smucker, who provided research assistance, and to Danita Greaser, who typed and proofread the majority of the poems in the manuscript. Grants from the Office of the Dean at Goshen College and the Women's Studies Program provided funds for permissions.

I owe a special thanks to my parents, John and Beulah Stauffer Hostetler, for introducing me to the rich heritage of Amish and Mennonite peoples, for giving me examples of scholarly rigor, and for showing me how books are made.

Most of all, I thank my husband, Merv Smucker, for support and understanding and our children, Elizabeth, Jonathan, Julia, and David, who graciously made space for this project in their lives over the past years.

Introduction
Mennonite Voices in Poetry

A cappella singing has been a time-honored tradition among Mennonites, from the unison hymns of the Reformation's historic Ausbund to the four-part harmony adapted from the singing school movement at the turn of the twentieth century. Voices, unaccompanied by other instruments, harmonize in a spiritual expression of community through music, a form of unadorned singing that has been one of the few consistent artistic traditions among Mennonites since the Reformation. This anthology heralds the flourishing of a new and vital literary movement among poets from Mennonite origins. The voices of the poets in this anthology, unlike those that blend in the singing of hymns, are distinctive and individual. But their conjoined presence in this volume creates a concert that reflects a varied legacy from Mennonite faith and culture.

Until the past decade or so, most of these poets wrote in isolation, unaccompanied by the affirmation of their various religious communities or even conversation with one another. But as poets from Mennonite contexts have emerged to gain literary recognition, they have gained a broad spectrum of readers — including, but not limited to, other Mennonites. The emergence of this poetry has begun to transform the ways in which contemporary Mennonites understand their own faith and culture. For a broader audience, this poetry offers Mennonite experience as a distinctive lens through which to view the universal themes that underlie all good poetry.

WHO ARE THE MENNONITES?

Mennonites are members of a historic peace church rooted in the Christian faith. As part of the Radical Reformation, Mennonites placed loyalty to God above loyalty to the state. Two of their most threatening practices to non-Mennonites were believer's (adult) baptism and the rejection of military service. Thus Mennonites were intensely persecuted by Protestants and Catholics alike. This legacy of persecution has had a complex effect on the development of Mennonites as a subculture. Initially both a rural *and* an urban movement among educated people — some early Anabaptists were students of the scholar and freethinker Desiderius Erasmus and his student Glarean — Mennonites soon were driven into the hinterlands, where they hid in small communities that worshipped together. Most Mennonites, as they immigrated to safer places — whether Pennsylvania at the invitation of William Penn or the steppes of Russia at the invitation of Catherine the Great — became a rural people renowned for their skills as artisans and agriculturalists.

The agricultural setting, combined with a strong community ethic and the tendency to separate from "the world," has until the mid twentieth century insulated Mennonites from mainstream fine arts. In addition, most Mennonites have been suspicious of the fine arts ever since their sixteenth-century ancestors rejected the signs and symbols of church art. History, for them, has taken precedence over fiction as a form of truth. Furthermore, art seems to compete with the centrality of the biblical text. Although music has been the most accepted art form, some groups still have a prohibition against musical instruments in their worship services.

During the latter half of the twentieth century, Mennonites have witnessed a number of radical changes. The half a million Mennonites in North America have been exceeded by the growing Mennonite populations in Africa, Asia, and South America. During America's civil rights movement and the Vietnam War era, many Mennonites became far more politically engaged in the struggle for peace and justice, joining others outside their denomination with similar goals. Mennonite colleges and higher education in general, as well as Mennonites migration from rural to urban settings, have opened the Mennonite Church to growth, change, global connection, and a young but vital arts movement.

One of the challenges that Mennonite poets offer to their community is how to *be* in the world. Traditionally Mennonites have considered themselves to be "in the world but not of it." Poetry, on the other hand, is rooted in the senses. It tends to connect rather than to separate. It privileges individual voice and vision in a context where mutual accountability and the discipline of the group have been primary. The poets in this volume challenge these separations as they celebrate body and voice, provoking new ways of seeing the world.

HOW THIS ANTHOLOGY CAME TO BE

In the spring of 1989 I was invited to join a group of other graduate students and writers to have lunch with Galway Kinnell, a guest poet at the University of Pennsylvania. As dishes were cleared and coffee cooled, the subject abruptly shifted to Mennonites and one of Kinnell's promising graduate students, a Mennonite named Julia Spicher (now Kasdorf). My thoughts raced.

Spicher? The only Spichers I knew were Mennonites who lived in Big Valley, a remote rural valley of central Pennsylvania where my father grew up as an Amish boy. How could a Spicher have found her way from a back-country farm town whose biggest enterprise was Peachey's Meats to the M.F.A. program at New York University, a prestigious poetry award, and book publication? My gut wrenched. Wanting to keep my own Mennonite identity inconspicuous, I said nothing.

As poet Deb Burnham, who had been Spicher's teacher at the Governor's School for the Arts, traded glowing stories about her with Kinnell, another distinguished poet at the table interjected, "Mennonites? Aren't they the people who refuse to vaccinate their children?"

My palms began to sweat. I usually tried to pass as a "nondescript Protestant" in the outside world. Outsiders seemed only to remember extreme stories about Mennonites; coming out to outsiders about one's Mennonite origins required elaborate historical and theological explanations that seemed to confound instead of illuminate. The offending poet, referring to an outbreak of measles in Pennsylvania a year or two earlier, which the media had traced to a fringe sect of nonvaccinating conservative Amish, was making a common blunder. Mennonites are all too often conflated or confused with a large variety of "plain peoples," all of whom have distinct beliefs and practices.

I had the urge to pull out my flawless immunization record and the flawless immunization records of every Mennonite I was related to. Instead, I kept my mouth shut. From experience I had learned that the power of preconception was too strong to be countered by reality. Soon everyone at the table would be asking me whether I drove a horse and buggy. I watched Kinnell and Burnham go to bat for Mennonites, or at least for Spicher. "Kasdorf, actually — she got married," corrected Kinnell. "But I like Spicher," he said. "Spike has character."

After the luncheon, I privately confessed my Mennonite identity to Burnham, who knew something about Mennonites, if only through Kasdorf's poetry. She also gave me some clues as to how Kasdorf had gotten from Belleville, Pennsylvania, to New York City. Although she spent the first year of her life in the rural community described in her book *Sleeping Preacher*, and evoked for me by the name Spicher, she had actually grown up in suburban Pittsburgh and attended a large public high school and the Governor's School for the Arts. Like many Mennonites growing up in the 1960s and 1970s, she was part of a family making the transition from a rural community to the complexity of urban and suburban life. Instead of being nurtured solely in a community of like-minded Mennonites as a fledgling writer, Kasdorf negotiated multiple communities, discourses, loyalties, even identities — as do the majority of Americans in our postmodern culture. Unwittingly, I had echoed the other poet's error when responding to her maiden name and community in terms of stereotype. I wondered how Kasdorf dealt with her Mennonite identity when coming up against the misunderstandings of her heritage. Unlike me, she seemed so unapologetic, so dispassionately curious about the marvelous details and particularities of the culture that was her heritage.

Years later I heard her explain to a group of students how she had written her much-anthologized poem "Mennonites." As a member of a graduate poetry-writing seminar at New York University, she sensed a strong but invisible difference in herself. In order to understand this difference — what it felt like to be Mennonite — she wrote this poem, anthologized here, with its earnest references to stories of martyrdom and hardship undercut by ironic overtones.

Kasdorf's poem, however, while it draws on images from both Russian and Swiss strands of Mennonites, two historically different groups, is not truly representative of all Mennonites. No poem can give a complete view of all Mennonites because the term "Mennonite" encompasses an increasing variety. In fact, her poem has provoked two very different responses from poets in this anthology — Jeff Gundy's "How to Write the New Mennonite Poem" and David Wright's "A New Mennonite Replies to Julia Kasdorf" — the first suspicious of poets who declare their Mennonite identity through images of folk traditions and artifacts, the second joining new practices and images to more traditional ones.

WHO ARE MENNONITE POETS?

A question I have wrestled with throughout the creation of this anthology is who are Mennonite poets? In order to qualify as a Mennonite poet for this anthology, a writer needs to meet one of the following criteria: be born into and/or be nurtured by one of the diverse groups whose designation includes the word "Mennonite" (in Canada alone there are twenty-five distinct groups of Mennonites), be a member of or regularly attend a Mennonite congregation, or be raised by or strongly influenced by close family relatives who are Mennonite. Thus I have tried to make the designation of "Mennonite poet" as broad as possible. Rather than attempt to define a voice that is distinctively Mennonite, I have sought to gather a sampling of the best work from a wide range of poets. The result is, I hope, a collection that reflects a diverse spectrum of sensibility informed by Mennonite experience — from outright rejection to vibrant and ongoing faith.

Several years after encountering Kasdorf's poetry, I attended a weekend festival of the arts sponsored by the Cincinnati Mennonite Fellowship. There I met both Kasdorf and poet Jeff Gundy and for the first time heard Canadian poet David Waltner-Toews read his "Tante Tina" poems in a Russian Mennonite–inflected Plautdeitsch, opening up an expression of Mennonite ethnicity unfamiliar to my own Swiss Mennonite experience. I also learned about the "Mennonite(s) Writing in the U.S." conference to be held at Goshen College in Goshen, Indiana, in the fall of 1997. This was my first inkling that Mennonite poets weren't as rare as I had previously thought. I realized that a community of writers was forming among Mennonites. From Kasdorf and Gundy I found out about the established community of Mennonite writers in Canada and the first Conference on Mennonite/s Writing in Canada, initiated by the *New Quarterly*, at the University of Waterloo in 1990, where a few of the U.S. Mennonite poets met each other as well as Canadian writers for the first time.

Encountering these writers and learning about others caused me to wish for an anthology of Mennonite poetry. How different my sense of myself as a writer and a Mennonite might have been if I had had access to such evidence of a vital literary tradition among the people of my faith and culture. What would it be like if I could explain Mennonites in terms of our poets instead of shopworn symbols such as coverings, the family farm, or moon pies? Gradually I decided, as Toni Morrison has said of her novels, to create the book — in this case the anthology — I was longing to read.

One of the great privileges of this project was being able to read hundreds of poems from far more poets than could be included in this volume. I hope that this anthology will inspire readers to seek out the works of individual poets and to become acquainted with a body of literature whose richness and breadth is barely suggested in the following pages. The selections are arranged by poet, and the poets are arranged chronologically by date of birth. I chose this method of organization so that it was possible to get a sense of development. The anthology seeks to combine the best writing from both U.S. and Canadian writers. The distinctive Canadian Mennonite literary community, which coalesced during the 1970s and 1980s, emerged before — and in many cases inspired — Mennonite poetry in the United States. As I compiled the anthology I discovered among the variety of styles and images some common themes: the relationship of individual to community; the tension between the authority of the community and the integrity of individual experience; the longing to break free of rigid patterns; the desire to juxtapose, if not synthesize, contradictions; and an emphasis on the sensuous and sensory world.

Above all, the poets in this anthology bring various realms of experience into dialogue, or even collision, with one another. Instead of joining in unison or even four-part harmony, the blending of their voices sounds more like the textured music of contemporary choral performance in which a leader gives several tones and the members of the choir improvise their own songs based on a spontaneous interpretation of scale or key. While it is impossible for the listener of such experimental and improvisational music to detect a single melody, the overall effect is something like a multilayered musical conversation with infinitely multiplying dimensions, perhaps a new image of singing in heaven.

A Cappella

Anna Ruth Ediger Baehr

Anna Ruth Ediger was born in 1916 in Clinton, Oklahoma, to General Conference Mennonite missionaries to the Southern Cheyenne. The sixth of eight children, she spent her first eighteen years accompanying her parents in their work and maintained her connection with the Cheyenne throughout her adult life. At Bethel College in North Newton, Kansas, she majored in home economics and met her future husband, Karl Baehr. The Baehrs then moved to Chicago, where they lived for nine years and where their two children were born. Another move took them to Long Island, New York, where Baehr spent the remainder of her life in Garden City.

Baehr finished her B.A. and earned an M.A. at Hofstra University, then taught elementary school for twenty-four years, much of the time supporting her family as her husband lost his eyesight. While she wrote poetry throughout her life, she began her serious involvement with poetry after her retirement from teaching in 1978. She served as coeditor of the literary magazine *Xanadu* for nine years and was coeditor of Pleasure Dome Press. The recipient of a New York State Creative Artists Program Service Award, she was also awarded the Mary Elinore Smith Poetry Prize by the *American Scholar* for her poem "I Am Dancing with My Mennonite Father" (1985). Her poetry also appeared in the *Long Island Poetry Review, Xanadu, Poetry Review, Kansas Quarterly*, and *West Hills Review* and was recorded by Choice Listening for the Blind. Baehr read her poetry on the radio and at fine arts centers, churches, schools, universities, and festivals, including Cheyenne celebrations. In her poetry collection, *Moonflowers at Dusk* (1996), she acknowledges the support of "the Long Island poetry community," especially George Wallace and David Ignatow. She died on June 24, 1998.

I Am Dancing with My Mennonite Father

We dance a carnival ride:
you try to make me feel
in your arms the thrust and turn
of the Ferris wheel, to give me
at last that ride I wanted long ago,
that you denied because you saw
my small body sway to gypsy rhythm,
my feet move in forbidden ways.

Under trellises we dance the leaves
I pinned on my friends' costumes
in third grade — *Welcome, Sweet
Springtime* — the garlands
I helped the teacher place
on their heads, backstage.

"It is all right," you say,
and I see how young you are,
how your damp hair curls.
But this is my fantasy. I should
tell you it is all right now.
I am no longer eight years old
in my modest dress watching you
in your black suit at the classroom
door tell the teacher that I am not
allowed to dance.

You move back to see my silhouette
against the light. "It is all right,"
I say, wind moving the sheer, forbidden
gown — all right to look at the outlines
of my body, to tell me by your smile
that other men will find me beautiful.

We dance all gossamer things,
not even trying to keep our feet
on the ground. You whisper now,
as you never did, "You're lovely,
and strong," spin me down patio steps
to the path, and let me go.

Cleaning the Cistern

Mother disappeared below the rim
in wraparound and ruffled cap,
holding the rope with one hand,
waving her brush with the other.

The next time Father lowered
the knotted rope, I stood
in the pail at its end and watched
the landscape turn slowly

into a shimmering disk,
then vanish, a talisman lost.
In the cool half-light,
in dappled shadow grays,

the smooth sunglinted walls
and dark pool played our voices.
We dipped brushes, scrubbed,
sent up dregs, received fresh water.

Mother laughed when we almost fell
on the sloping floor. I talked
of living in the Underworld,
abandoned, wondering who above

would care enough to find us.
Dancing around the small
now sun-bright pool,
holding our brushes high,

we felt wise and told each other
we needed no one else.
When every inch was clean,
even our boots washed and dry

for the last steps underground,
the cloths and brushes already
hauled above, I shouted
for the pail, my voice

fractured into bits
that circled and bounced.
Take me last, I called and saw
my mother ascend, her skirt

blocking light. For an instant, the dread
inside a smooth underground flask,
alone, hope a hole to the sky
beyond my reach.

Ritual

I stand beside the gate, alone, deep
in lilacs that sweeten the corral, and watch
a bull against a large moon, the head black
in silhouette, a rise of silver washing
over him, over the dewy field, over me.
Quiet, violence forgotten, we are as close
as we were a few hours earlier, running
across a field I did not know was his.
I touch the gauze covering bloody cuts
of barbed wire on my arms and back,
remembering the dark shape behind me,
the bellow, how my breath came hard,
no time to part the wires far enough.

Now we dream by the same moon, the bull
poised like some god gentled at night, blood
cooled. He turns his head to me. I stare
into the approaching shadow, stretch my hand
through the fence, and stroke the side
of his face, soft and warm in the marbled
darkness. He holds still, and I feel
the terrible hardness, bones under flesh.

In another age I might have stood beneath
an altar to receive blood from his sacred
throat. I tuck night-paled lilacs
into the waxy strap around his neck.

I want to touch the horns, but he turns
away. Glints of moonlight lead the hulking
blackness into the violet night.

I Will Not Pretend

---

for my Southern Cheyenne friends

I will not pretend
that I can see with your eyes,
that I hear in the drum all you hear.
I see with my own eyes,
but I look where you look,
listen for the same sounds,
and answer to the name you gave me.

I know your streams, from
the Mississippi to Turtle Creek.
In forests and groves I find your trees,
though I do not point them out
to everybody. On my plain are clusters
of tipis and distant herds of buffalo.
The crier calls, I smell woodfires
and go to the big tent.

These things are part of me
just as are the secret
meeting places in Holland, fields
of grain in Russia, the ancient
pitcher in Grandmother's kitchen,
the books on my father's shelves.

I am not two people,
but I have two peoples.
If I have sometimes seemed to deny this,
it is because there has been a great
distance. I have called to one, then
to the other, facing two ways,
not knowing that I must see both
at the same time lest I be divided
within myself, lose part of myself.

You have welcomed me, offered me
a place again in my first home.
I have returned. I am here.

Christina

Her brothers take turns reading to her
at bedtime — stories about giants, fairies,
forests as thick as a moonless night, oceans
that can float ships and dragons,
someone who used wings his father made
and flew too close to the sun,

                    God,
who didn't like what people were doing
so he sent his son down to be killed.

                    And Satan,
whom an angel with a trumpet will bind
when the last days come. It isn't clear
just where the angel will tie the devil.
Christina hopes it will not be a post
in the fence around her house.

She knows about the last days:
something about the sky when all-over clouds
thicken and close in at sunset with no sun
but a dense threatening reddish glow,
then darkness.

Or when green-gray clouds bring
the smell of storm and make Christina
feel the little hairs on her neck as she
follows her family down to the cellar,
where they will probably be when
the world ends.

Or what comes next: an opening in the sky,
clouds parting as they do in pictures
of the Second Coming, a shining
that makes the hole so bright Christina
is sure

                    Jesus
will float through, holding out his hands.

She knows about God, how he spies
on us, always closer than any real
person can be, even when we try
to keep a secret or when we
go to the bathroom.

She knows about

                    God,
how he was lonely so he made people
who look like him. He insists
we have to love him even if we
don't like him. He is like

                    a father
who holds you on his lap and tells you
to pray and when you refuse
he puts you facedown on his fat knees
and hits you and makes you drop your doll.

God talks to some people, but not
to Christina, and that makes her mad.
God should be at least as loud
as a giant, as

                    her father
when he yells. When she
complains, someone tells her about

                    the still, small voice.
Nobody could ever be quieter than
Christina when she really tries.
She sits with her hands folded in her lap,
eyes closed, listening.

She hears
the tick of a grandfather clock,
her mother humming,
and — through an open window — a distant
train and a song sparrow.

Jane Rohrer

Jane Turner, born in 1928 in Broadway, Virginia, grew up on a large farm where her father raised Tennessee walking horses. Although her father had a somewhat tempestuous relationship with the local congregation, her mother was a devout member of the church. Jane attended Eastern Mennonite High School for four years and spent two years at Eastern Mennonite College (now Eastern Mennonite University). At college, she met her husband, Warren Rohrer, who later became a painter of national renown.

After Jane and Warren were married in 1948, the Rohrers moved to Philadelphia, where Warren studied at the Pennsylvania Academy of the Fine Arts and where their sons, Jon and Dean, were born. The Rohrers drifted away from the Mennonite Church as their lives became increasingly centered in the art world, although they maintained lifelong friendships with a circle of friends who had a Mennonite background and a strong interest in the arts. In 1961 they bought a farm outside Philadelphia in Christiana, Pennsylvania, and lived there for the next twenty years. Warren painted and Jane gardened and began to write poetry.

In the early 1970s, when their sons left home, Jane began reading and writing poetry intensively. She then studied poetry writing with Stephen Berg (University of the Arts) and Thomas Kinsella (Temple University) and began publishing her work. Eight of her poems appeared in the *American Poetry Review* between 1977 and 1985. After Warren was diagnosed with chronic lymphocytic leukemia in 1979, the Rohrers sold their farm and moved back to Philadelphia. Jane wrote less during the next fifteen years until Warren's death in 1995. She has recently published new work in the *American Poetry Review* and her first book of poems, *Life after Death*. Her work has been anthologized in *The Body Electric: America's Best Poems from the American Poetry Review*, edited by Stephen Berg et al., and in *Parallels: Artists/Poets*, edited by Grace Gluck.

In the Kitchen before Dinner

The winter sky past the feeder,
Beyond the wood of straight trees
And the field rising to the ridge,
Is unnervingly delicate.
But you are acquainted with the country
And you know poems. You've heard this.

Years, years and years, I've looked out
From this window, stirring —
      Straight out of the sun
      a cardinal swoops to the feeder,
      his sweep, not his shape,
      the unstrokable wing of art.
Seeing that,
I want to tell you:
      The sun of poems is on the snow
      on the slope past the wood
      to the pond. What I see at 5:00.
      It marries the music from my living room.
      It is not that simple.
      I cannot explain it.
Saying that,
I think I cannot ever leave.
I'm grounded by attachment, I'm rapacious
For facts: That bowl.
      His gloves on the chair
      holding each other.
These I can explain.

Mennonite Funeral in the Shenandoah Valley

I could never reach this place
But for a memory of Christmas that plays
At the edge of the winter in my mind.

Beside me in the long hallway my father chokes softly.
He's down now from the black horse
      and the worldly track he rode
      in widening circles
      away from her.
This is her day.
In the front parlor she has drawn her Circle around her.
Still and unreachable, she receives
The favored.   (So nice of you to come.)

Outside, on the curved driveway,
We must all fit somehow on this natural occasion.
My aunts, her secular sisters, sit in black cars
Smoothing on their gloves
Finger by inspected finger.
In the way of things I wait with him
In some other black car until
The column uncouples, a wake behind her bell-coach
Inching ahead. Soundless we creep
          we crawl to the last place
          and couple obedient in line.
We wait. I listen. The pines keep sighing.
I remember them. They always sighed.
The reach.
They aspire.

More of her people wait. (So nice of you to come.)
She gains the Plain doorway, that eye of needle,
Moves regal up the gray aisle, under pink roses,
Without her crutch. Wait.
This room is a strangled room, that clock
Is choking.
Mustiness lingers in odor of pamphlet and Sunday vest,

The light is unstained, cut into blocks on the cold floor.
We, the uneven hem of her earthly garment,
Are pleated to fit the short front pew.
Breath. I cannot breathe this death. I hear
The varnished pulpit say, "Dearly Beloved
And you who left the faith
And this saint."

Her pink fragrance is paling now
And this is bitter bread, O day in my sweet life. "Go-in Home
Go-in Home."

I take my place with her unforgiven
see her folded
into that satin cathedral. O strange return
O train up a child
O child

The Gearshift Poem

If I look at his hand on the gearshift
My thighs will open
My palm will settle to his thick wrist
Feel which way to move
Down the back of his hand to the skin tip
Up his sleeve to rough
Jacket shoulder shirt neck hair black bouncing
To my hand sending
Messages to my whole self here in the
Car after twenty
Eight years it is still happening —
If his hand ever
(Now gliding level first to window
Then to radio)
Lights I will stroke it thinking yes
And wanting not to cage him in habit.

Room 703

I see now you were rehearsing death
that day at the University of Pennsylvania Hospital.
I thought it was just a continuation
of our 46 year conversation
and that, since you could no longer paint,
you had turned poet.

You spoke from a vast white prairie of bed,
a place with no direction:
"It's Mr. Alexander."
"Who is Mr. Alexander?" I asked.
You answered, *"This thing inside me.*
He's a gnome-like creature with a large head.
We are co-owners of an ocean-going vessel."

When I opened the curtains and windows
to the clear space above the city,
again you spoke, as though saying something important:
"You know that saying, between a rock and a hard place?
Well, it should be put in a box on a high shelf
and brought out only for an occasion like this."

My end of the conversation hung in my throat.
Some hard place.
We could simply wait for Mr. Alexander
to come in his vessel
or we could go out on intravenous tubes.

And what did I mean, we?

For the third year
on the day of his death
I left my house on a hopeful journey
to Rhoads Pavilion
and the purr of an elevator
large and posh enough to move into.
There I was again to visit.

I walked straight ahead
past the closed door of Room 703,
past the nurses' station,
lest someone say, *"May I help you?"*
and I answer, *"Where have you put him?"*

Hotel

You have been gone for years
   yet I live with you.
Nights are best
   because of the dreams,
   bridging as they do
   the dimensions
   of this three-dimensional chessboard
   we move upon.

Take the night we met
   in the hotel of before and after.
It was almost too far for you to come
   but you were happy
   and had a message.
I see my hand click the lock
   and hear the click
   and say, "We haven't a moment to lose."

And we danced.
We danced a dance we had never learned,
   coming as we did from people
   who applied themselves diligently
   to the practice of refraining from dance.
Anyway, I will never forget it.
Once we got the hang of it,
   it was way beyond anything
   from our loveliest days, don't you think?

Even so,
   so insubstantial was its perfection,
   the old flawed days haunt
   and the memory of material mesmerizes.
I say bodybody.

Stopping by Fields on a Snowy Afternoon

You have obviously been here
   since my last visit
   and I like what you've done.
But, is it landscape
   or is it art?
It's all so confusing
   with you coming from the other side.

Calligraphy, there on the contours of the field,
   scribbling in stalks and stacks
   left from the fall,
   are visible in the distant upper levels
   of the canvas.
If it is a canvas.
But, it's the wash of thin white,
   just a sift of snow
   (or is it white)
   that erases the visual samsara
   and beckons to me from beyond the pale.
But I can't.
I am per pale.

We've been split like a schist.
Here I am and there you are,
   parallel.

Sarah Klassen

Sarah Klassen was born in Winnipeg, Manitoba, in 1932 and grew up on a farm in the interlake region of Manitoba ("Bush Country") until her family moved back to Winnipeg so she could attend the Mennonite Brethren Collegiate Institute. She received her B.A. and B.Ed. from the University of Manitoba and attended the Mennonite Brethren Bible College for two years. At first an elementary school teacher, Klassen moved to high school teaching at River East Collegiate in Manitoba, where she taught for twenty-five years. Since 1990 she has devoted herself full time to writing, with several sojourns to Lithuania and the Ukraine as a teacher of English literature and language. Always an avid reader, Klassen describes a "long apprenticeship" in the classroom that led her to a close study of poetry and the short story. Her first collection of poetry, *Journey to Yalta* (1988), won the Gerald Lampert Memorial Award for the best first book of the year. Her second book, *Violence and Mercy*, was nominated for the Pat Lowther Award and the McNally Robinson Award for Manitoba Book of the Year. Her third volume, *Borderwatch*, contains poems inspired by her work in Lithuania. *Dangerous Elements* and *Simone Weil: Songs of Hunger and Love*, her fourth and fifth volumes of poetry, respectively, underscore her importance as a major figure on the Canadian literary scene. In 2000 she received the National Magazine Award, Gold, for poetry.

Klassen is a member of the River East Mennonite Brethren Church in Winnipeg, a congregation supportive of the arts. She has been editor (1992–1995) of *Sophia*, a magazine by and for Mennonite women. As a member of the feminist caucus of the League of Canadian Poets, she has served as editor of *Women and Violence* and contributed to *Siolence: Poets on Women, Violence, and Silence*. She is a member of the Manitoba Writers' Guild and the League of Canadian Poets. Her poetry has been set to music, and some of her writing has been influenced by contemporary women's art.

Act of Mercy

My mother killed cats
that winter the farm was vacated
chickens shipped
crated to the slaughter house
oats and barley bagged, granaries
swept clean. Even the rats
vanished.

       That January
temperatures fell to forty
below for a whole week.
My father's coffin blurred
in a blizzard, the sharp snow
burning our faces.

All her life my mother believed
nothing was easy. Coming home
I found her in my father's fading
torn coat and winter boots
bent over empty feed troughs. The price
of eggs still sinking the day
I stumbled on the iron-hard
bodies of the cats she'd stuffed
with mittened hands, warm
into a gunny sack.

Russian Fables

My mother sings me a song
in Russian, murmurs about pigs, acorns,
a wise black crow in an oak
tree she remembers from a fable
by Krylov.

Whenever the ending eludes her
she begins again.
I who have heard this fable
all my life, recite the moral
quoting the black crow.

My mother says *Nothing
is in vain*. The pain stabbing her
swollen joints, crushed bones of her spine
fallen away like scales on the cobbled road

through Barvenkovo: the village
schoolroom where the Czar reigns
sternly over scrubbed faces
of Mennonite children reciting
without error the Cyrillic alphabet,
the gospel stories, old
fables in Russian. His own children learn

those same fables
can't save them from brute force
of bayonets, the steel-cold
mystery of dying.
The terrible, unbroken dark.

Mennonite children are saved,
good or bad. They sail across a blue ocean
to a golden land where they begin again:
a brand new alphabet. Meadowlarks and wind
singing through prairie grass
blur the distant rattle of machinegunfire,
the last faint wail of dying
children. My mother's stubborn

gratitude outlasts all anger,
every memory,
the somber squawking of the crow.
It silences the pain clamped like a chain
around her milk-white limbs.

She sings to me in Russian,
her voice a thread, a thin road winding
its fabulous, oak-shadowed way
relentlessly
though Barvenkovo.

Artist and Medium

Martyrdom like radiance of a clear night sky
can leave you baffled. Jan Luyken finds no words for it
although he's written love lyrics, painted
morning and evening in pale tones. He knows

delicate brush strokes can't take hold of this
triumphant dying: a song torn from between charred lips
the way a sword's torn from the heart.
Jan chooses a needle and begins

dribbling acid on a copper plate. He's pleased
with the austerity of etching the fine line
between agony and exultation,
between silence and breath. He tries defining

faith: should it be modest or bold,
reasonable, fervent, fanatical? He's drawn to the plain
homeliness of bound hands
and feet, a stretched wrist, bones stripped clean

the raw texture of freshly seared skin. He's engraved
the afternoon mob taunting the condemned
for heresy, the executioner
for a job badly done.

He's mastered the way the greedy flames reach out
for flesh, a child's hand
for its doomed mother, the impatient soul
ecstatically for God.

Repenting

If
at the last minute
(lascivious tongues of flame
licking your skin
caressing your quivering arms and legs)

you suddenly want to live
not die
not for the whole world
not even for Almighty God's
truth, what for God's sake can you do

lashed to the stake
your aching mouth screwed shut
blood pounding
hard as axe blows in your brain
and a breeze fanning the fire.

Blades of grass shudder.
Trees dissolve in smoke. Above you
the birdwings' muffled drumbeat
whispers the dirge: too late
too late   it's
too late.

Making the Rate (factory journals)

1.

Mornings I carve washers from bars of sheet metal at the large press
and drill a million or so holes in the heavy baffle plate.

Unless you maintain uninterrupted tempo they tell me you won't
make the rate. While cutting pieces out of brass strips at the heavy
press I botch fourteen. Leon claims the holes aren't centred right and
consequently I fail to make the rate.

In the afternoon at a machine operated with buttons I camber the pieces cut this morning, polish one thousand and eight parts at the stamping machine. No one tells me that unless you apply just the right pressure the pulley turns traitor and shifts and the belligerent belt rides off.

Once again I fail to make the rate.

2.

At the end of the morning a machine flails its raging limbs and with bare teeth tears a clump of hair completely from the head of a woman operating it.

In the afternoon the woman is back with a new hairnet. Hard not to stare at the naked spot, a round pale shining, and everyone labours to avoid her. She oils the snarling maniac machine, offers it complete attention and by evening succeeds in exceeding the rate.

3.

It's always a man sets up the press for a woman. The bastards believe they are masters of mechanical performance, know how hard to thrust, just when to bear down, hold back, the right timing and tempo. Their voices when they speak to you are hard as steel. Demands they make about position and control are beyond reason, beyond decency. In the heat of the furnace your arms and thighs drip with sweat. Your heart is a desperate hammer pounding in a hollow room.

4.

While considering Trotsky who never in his life stepped inside a factory I become careless and as a result a small tooth breaks from the saw. This is noticed by the foreman who informs the timekeeper who enters figures on a chart.

Marx and God are problems best abandoned when you're trying desperately to make the rate.

5.

Nenette's friend makes love to a painter morning noon and night.
She hints at getting paid and analyzes gladly his techniques in detail
for anyone who asks. Evidently she's deprived of nothing and spends
her spare time cooking and eating.

Mimi whose sister owns a house in the suburbs tells jokes that would
make a regiment of Hussars blush.

The Italian woman is ill and Mouquet has refused leave.
Eugenie says a collection will be taken for Madame Forestier.
Josephine and the redhead vow they will give nothing. Nenette and
the Italian woman refuse too.

Nenette weeps over coffee, speaking with love of her son who is
clever and likes to read. She swears she'll shelter him with her
exhausted body, save him with her hungry years from martyrdom
and workshops. Tears flood her eyes, her work-worn hands are steel-
tight fists.

In spite of the anger smouldering behind half-lowered eyelids, words
boiling over, it's cold in the cloakroom where we huddle in our brief,
uneasy sisterhood. I bite my tongue to keep from speaking. If I had
tears they would fall warm for Nenette.

6.

Today I achieve a rapid cadence which leads to an acceptable tempo
which I sustain for several hours and I make the rate and know for a
moment standing close to the drilling press a delirious fraternity. A
kind of mechanical joy.

7.

I believe workers if they knew the principles of pulleys and
crankshafts, the clear meaning of force and counterforce, if they were
taught to master the mathematics of machines, logic of transmission
belts, they would be filled with proud joy, infused with such spirit
the revolution would flare out like a pasque flower and France would
at last be free.

Toward evening the clumsy nitwit setting my machine catches his left
thumb in a clamp. The bastard bawls out like an ox. His blood drips
random patterns on the sea of perfect washers I have polished.

8.

When I count them the round pieces the machine has pressed out
slip through my fumbling fingers forcing me to begin again. I can
never be sure the final tally is true and what I take home in my
pocket in pay determines my true worth as a worker.

I who draw intricate analogies between mathematics and Christ,
mediator between the world and God, am lost in the sheer number
of metal pieces either perfect or spoiled. My misery is absolute. I
bring it home with me daily: a shrill buzzing in my head and a deep
aching that will not let me sleep.

9.

At the end of the day I come to the Seine River where I sit exhausted
on a stone wall. The silent water as I watch it speaks an invitation so
dark and urgent my numb body and my lacerated spirit want to say
yes yes.

In the nick of time, remembering the foreman, I order my unwilling
feet to move and march me quickly across the bridge.

10.

When the bus stops for me and the driver lets me board I'm amazed
knowing I've been made a slave and like all slaves have no place
anywhere. The whole way I wait for the voice that will order me off.
The rough shove of an arm.

At night I lie sleepless on the hard floor and weep for the kindness of
the driver.

And if I sleep I dream: machines whining, clanking steel on steel, the
hollow thud of the large press grinding piece after piece of
humiliation from strips of brass copper tin. The compressed air
drill clamps me to its breast and we become one body, the incessant
vibration as we dance alien to the soul's rhythm.

A giant hammer beating in my brain.

11.

For once I succeed in replacing free thought with bitterness. The
energy thus generated drives me to achieve unusual speed. No
spoiled pieces and when I make the rate Leon has nothing to say.

12.

I daydream all day at the machine not bothering to return tools. Botched pieces are concealed, the final tally fabricated. Lunchtime I eat my fill of bread and sausage, drink glass after glass of red wine and offer hand-rolled cigarettes, my last, to Mimi and Nenette.

Jean Janzen

Jean Wiebe grew up on the prairie, moving from Dalmeny, Saskatchewan, where she was born in 1933, to Mountain Lake, Minnesota, in 1939 and later to Kansas when her schoolteacher father became a pastor. During her formative years, Jean, the seventh of eight children, absorbed the landscape, her father's sermons, her mother's love of music, and the stories of her Russian Mennonite past. She studied at Meade Bible Academy, Tabor College, and Grace College before marrying Louis Janzen and moving with him to Chicago, where she took courses at Northwestern University and worked as a medical secretary while Louis trained as a pediatrician. After his residency they moved to Fresno, California, where they raised four children. Jean Janzen earned her B.A. at Fresno Pacific University and taught piano for many years before turning to poetry as her primary artistic focus. Janzen earned an M.A. in creative writing and English from California State University at Fresno, where she studied with Peter Everwine and Philip Levine. She also counts Mennonite novelist Rudy Wiebe as an important mentor and influence on her career as a writer.

Over a hundred of Janzen's poems have appeared in a wide range of literary and religious periodicals, from *Poetry*, *Prairie Schooner*, and the *Gettysburg Review* to *Image*, *Christian Century*, and *Mennonite Life*. Her chapbook, *Words for the Silence*, published in a limited edition by the Center for Mennonite Brethren Studies in Fresno, explores the Russian Mennonite experience of her father and his family, including a grandmother whose suicide was shrouded in silence. Since her first book she has published four additional collections of poetry, most recently *The Snake in the Parsonage* and *Tasting the Dust*. In 1995 Janzen won a Creative Writing Fellowship from the National Endowment for the Arts. She taught creative writing at both Eastern Mennonite University and Fresno Pacific University. She is a charter member of the College Community Mennonite Brethren Church in Clovis, California.

These Words Are for You, Grandmother

i

I imagine you sitting on the doorstep,
your dark braid undone and rippling
down your back. You are plucking
melodies from the guitar which
he made for you, and he is there
singing along, his arm soft around you
in the Ukrainian dusk. And now it seems
that we are both entering the darkening
house to the pale bed, this bed
of beginnings and endings, of arms
encircling and then letting go,
this bed which you have given me
by your womb.

ii

The crude violin, the little organ
he made of wood scraps and animal bones,
and your guitar are all silent in the room,
the strings untouched. His long hand
slipped from yours after the last embrace,
after his last gathering of the nine
young faces around the terrible bed.
And then the cold light in the room
and the silence, and heaven so far away.
The ministers brought shoes for the children,
flour for your bin. But you were silent,
your eyes empty, your mouth still.
The photograph tells me that
I have eyes and hands like yours
and a mouth with a heavy lower lip.
Look, I am shaping it for words,
making sounds for you. I am speaking
the syllables you couldn't say.
See my breath is pushing away the cold.

iii

After you hanged yourself
they buried you outside the gate
without songs, just a prayer
in the harsh light. My father,
ten years old, had found you
in the barn, your body
a still dark strip, your face
swollen and purple. And by that grave
he could not sing for you;
he did not speak of you.
He sealed his mouth with a heavy stone
and walked away.
And when he held me in his arms
he spoke of rivers
and a black crow against the sky.
Helen of darkness,
I sing you a song.
It is like water from a clear stream,
like a white linen dress.
I take you down, wash you
and comb your hair.
I lay you down beside the man you loved.

iv

The small, abandoned graveyard
lies in tall autumn grass, the markers
tumbled and covered. Last grasshoppers
have gone from the nearby stubbled fields
and a light frost whitens the feathery
heads of foxtail. I have come down
the long narrow road. I have come
with my passport, my photograph
and my name to stand on the unmarked dust
of your body, and there is no sound
but the dry leaves stirring in the alders,
the groaning of roots, and these words
breathing on a page.

Chicken Guts

After the sticky steam of plums
and the fuzz of peaches, we caught chickens
in the yard, stewing hens for canning.
Dad with a hatchet on the old elm stump
and I in the cellar scraping grit out of gizzards.
All in a sort of ritual dance: the chop,
the boiling body-dip for defeathering, the swing
through the singe of fire. Then, disembowel, dismember.
All for the grand finale behind glass — a chorus line
of chicken legs caught in the kick, like a photo.
This is not about death, or violence to animals,
not even about sex. It's about those intestines
I stripped into the bucket. About how they
could have been saved, stretched across a hollow,
and made to sing. It's about my cousin Eugene
who plucks and saws the gut of his cello until
something throbs in our own. And it's about dance,
not the scratch and kick of the chicken's life,
but the deep stomp that awakens the bottom
of the lake, the dance I want to do among
the festival of wild grass and flowers back
in my hometown. I want to lean low,
to paint my face with mulberry juice
and stay up all night. I want to put my ear
against the belly of the earth to hear
it rumble, to hear it sigh.

How They Loved

Inside each of us lies the secret
of our parents. We carry it

like a small stone buried
and glimmering — how they loved

under the layered pressures
and the scouring of days, the stream

singing over them. Hidden.
But sometimes we catch a glimpse

inside a darkened room where a pair
of glassblowers work beside the furnace-

glow. They shape a vessel
with their breaths, the dance

of their bodies, and the firing.
They hold it up to the lamp,

turning it. "See how strong," they say,
and test it on the old brick floor

where it rolls, whole, in that other
country we hold inside of us, where some days

they stroll together in a city square,
bright with mist under the sliding sun.

Wild Grapes

Grandfather, dying in November,
asked for wild grapes from
a distant creek. He remembered them,
sweet under the leaves, sent Peter,
his eldest, on horseback.
Through the window the light,
golden as broth, filled his bedside cups,
and the dusty air shimmered.

I have known others who, at the end,
crushed the flesh of nectarine against
the dry palate, or swallowed bits
of cake, eyes brimming.

What to drink in remembrance
of each morning that offered itself
with open arms? What food
for the moments we whispered
into its brightness?

Grandfather, the last pain-filled days,
dreamed cures. He who loved God,
who would go to him, but who also
loved this world, filled as it is
with such indescribable beauty,
you have to eat it.

Claiming the Dust

Like nomads we come
to this subtropical valley,
our borrowed space
under the sun. Once
an ancient lakebed,
the July ground powders
under our feet, lifts
in puffs to welcome us.
The children rise, then
run out to pound acorns
under the oaks, calling
to each other from
their rings of stones.
Pale bird-of-paradise leans
out of its gravelly bed.
It takes dynamite to plant
an orange tree, our neighbor sighs.

This is our new home,
this valley's layered clay
which offers its sunbaked surface
to the scuffing of our feet,
as if our fragile lives
are enough to rouse the ages.
The slightest breeze, and the dust
becomes skittish, whirls
to settle in the next yard.
But mostly, stillness,

so that the beige siftings
are almost imperceptible.
Fig leaves in a talcum haze.

It is the night we finally learn
to claim. At dusk the children
float their sheets like flattened tents
and sprawl face-up into the warm
darkness, and we join them
in this rehearsal — a summer
night travel, the sky's black
curtains pinned back with stars.
That open stage.
This hard earth not our final holding
place after all, but the air
into which we sail,
breath by dusty breath,
toward a different shore.

Learning to Sing in Parts

After the quarrelling at recess
my father teaches his students
to listen, to hold a pitch and hum it,
his head close to the small child.

And the child listens and seeks
for the tone, sliding into a float
of singing, the whole room of children
riding out now on one note.

But then two, three, even four tones
at once, my father sorting and joining
their varied voices into a rich and layered
flow. How to hold against the other pitches?

This is the world's secret, he confides,
to enter and be close, yet separate.
That room musty with chalk and sweat, closed
door, and still the harmony slips out,

escaping like most secrets do. Alone
at the end of the day, the schoolhouse empty
and shadowed, my father wonders, can it
be taught? He seeks it too. How patiently

his own father taught him, held him close,
his voice vibrating light and low under
the wavering melody, a duet
that hovers over the stony fields.

Leonard Neufeldt

The twentieth-century migrations of Leonard Neufeldt's family reflect the complexity of the Russian Mennonite move to the Western Hemisphere: Neufeldt's paternal grandparents left Siberia for Mexico in 1925; in the following year they migrated to the Canadian province of Saskatchewan. His maternal grandparents migrated directly from Siberia to Saskatchewan in 1925. In 1929 these two families moved with several others to the frontier settlement of Yarrow, British Columbia, to join a Mennonite community begun less than a year earlier. Neufeldt was born there in 1937. His volumes of poetry from the 1990s, especially *Raspberrying* (1991) and *Yarrow* (1993), explore this community, which is also the subject of a two-volume cultural history, *Yarrow, British Columbia: Mennonite Promise* (2002), which he co-authored and edited. *Raspberrying* was nominated for the 1992 Governor General's Award for Poetry in Canada. More than 140 of his poems have appeared in numerous literary magazines and anthologies in both the United States and Canada, including the *Georgia Review*, *Michigan Quarterly Review*, *Poetry Northwest*, *Prairie Fire*, and *Sewanee Review*.

After Neufeldt completed a B.A. in English at Wilfred Laurier and a Ph.D. in English and history at the University of Illinois, he taught at the University of Washington, the University of Texas, and Purdue University. At Purdue, where he taught for twenty-two years until his retirement in 1999, he was professor of English and American studies, chaired American studies, and served as associate editor of the Purdue University Press poetry series. Through his poetry Neufeldt pays tribute to his Mennonite heritage and his Canadian roots, as well as conversing with other poets from Mennonite traditions. Neufeldt now lives with his wife, Mera, in Gig Harbor, Washington.

Dyke View Berry Farm

1.

Time couldn't take away our words but place changed them.
Words are a family trait. Our Mennonite ancestors —
teachers, traders, poets, garrulous
farmers, businessmen, brandymakers, musicians —
were mostly too poor or too suddenly rich
to stop talking, and everyone was spoken for
before he was born. Strange idioms
in a land as foreign as the Fraser Valley
made little difference. Father, a businessman
who studied music and dreamed of teaching choirs
that sang only pianissimo,
learned silence on his own
but it made no dent on his children,
and it didn't change the fact that in 1619
his tirelessly non-resistant Dutch forebears
forsook salt marshes, canals, dykes, orchards,
and waist-high grasses to do their talking,
singing, and praying out loud in Schleswig
while the Spanish armies broke the truce
and then the dykes and for the greater glory of God
gutted quivering fields and those
who stayed because they could not leave
or praising God too generously left too late.

2.

The year that Father kept everything to himself
he bought six open acres of hard bottom land
where the lower Chilliwack River, renamed the Vedder
and redirected, received the upper Chilliwack
from a high mountain valley and spilled into Sumas Lake.
Canada geese gathered like immigrants
to gabble by thousands among themselves
over water rights while the Fraser Valley
was subdivided from Yarrow, before it had a name,
to the northside wall of mountains the shade of blueprints

engineers had drawn of the Canal, the dykes
on either side gray lines, straight as raspberry rows.

3.

As our raspberry rows blossomed with a hum of bees
winter died eastward, mountain to mountain,
and the new President of the Yarrow Co-op
announced price hikes, a larger cannery,
and six tons per acre, crops palpable as geese
returning by thousands along the Vedder Canal
from the States, where the fresh-painted Co-op trucks
would soon again deliver twice a week
coopered whiskey barrels that leaked raspberry jam
down Highway 11 past the U.S.
Customs officers who waved them on excessively.

4.

Why ancestors left Holland was as important
to Father as history planted here and now
in rows, if possible, in soil one's bones claim as their own,
paid for before its yield is known, hard
as the clay of Dyke View Berry Farm.
The dyke silvering north and south
for miles of old lake bottom when the fog
rolled free of poplars and Vedder Mountain
and the sun; the earth hardening
to a gray slate before it turned grass green.

5.

Grasses grew everywhere in our berry rows,
sprouting, we swore, from the canes themselves.
We warred against wild grasses: five brothers,
hoes thudding like pheasants startled
from their nests, hoes made by our blacksmith,
Mr. Reimer, whose arms were hard as anvils,
who didn't know how hard our soil was because
Father didn't explain why he wanted heavy
blades made, and he never held a hoe

except to match handle to son. Our hoes bounced
with surprise as we argued with them,
as they sheared grasses that would grow again
and sometimes a berry plant that wouldn't;
sometimes the hoe wedged down to harder bottom,
a rock where it shouldn't have been,
and the back stiffened to say
"something too large to move,
something to build on."

6.

In our berry field Father wanted everything
to speak for itself: family name,
reclaimed lake and marshes, hardpan clay,
hymns chosen for Sunday, bumper crops,
another window broken in the pickers' cabins,
the unexpected death of the King,
pacifism, newly forged hoes.
Father, you rode your red tractor
through our shouts across the rows, our hoes,
backs, arms, and thin buttocks held tight
against wires and plants to let you by
singing Mendelssohn's *Elijah,* your left hand
conducting dustpan rows, your right
feeling the jabs of the wheel.
Only into the second chorus, your favorite, you drove
into the drainage canal: tractor — cultivator — harrow —
conductor's score. "No boys, the clutch failed."
You shook your trouser legs and music. We bent
to our work, begged the hard earth to bear us out
as we reached inward, dreaming of crop failures,
hungry for anything but raspberries.

The tree with a hole in our front yard

for Di Brandt, and to those who were angry

Some in Yarrow will tell it differently,
forests emptying, or holes
in the sky at the poles of our world
where we can lose everything.

For years our flowering chestnut
was a circle in our eye,
roundness so dark and unconditional
we didn't notice until our Oregon cousin
ripped it open after vomiting his gin,
rode the largest bough down to earth,
and let sky in as though
to prove it round,
but trees have holes gaping with disbelief.

When a boy knows he's failed to explain
a perfect circle to Father, and the sky opening,
he is silent about the vacancy within,
new and large, unhealable.
But the chestnut didn't die,
first one side of the gap and then the other,
to its last, outermost branch.

Some of us stood in the emptiness
long after it had healed over,
trying to remember
word for word what Father said,
as if a child's wonder or a father's answer
are magic. They are more like trees
or the sky seeking to close itself.

The man with the glass eye

That eye didn't stop Mr. Isaak
from beating boys for being too young,
anyone's boy, even his own.
He could close his smaller eye,
magnify those in front rows
who weren't listening,
and keeping them clearly focused
he'd shake his loose suit down the aisle
of the church like a tired grizzly,
scruff up a kid one-handed
as the hymn was being announced, hold him
frantic at arms length as though to read him
like a first stanza, and carry him out the side door
to cuff him. There's no telling
what will make a boy scream, whether it's more
than pain, or less, or how some growls
and sky-thin wailing will burst slowly
into a cadenza when the stanza comes to an end,
or why Mr. Isaak would return alone, swayed
by a pulse pressing on like waves,
water or earthquake, rows of them, boys
looking down at their hands as his eye went by.

Only once did a father separate his son
from that grip-long growl, send him back,
and shake Isaak's shoulders until the thing
fell out, and he helped him look for it
in the gravel,

that eye pressing forward day and night,
never needing sleep — so far beyond
repose that at night, we heard,
it popped impatiently out, rolled an inch
at a time past his slightly poised
hand near the edge and down
to the footend of the bed he slept in alone.
It would focus on him there.

That's what made him angry in the morning:
glass eye, monstrous nightshirt,
and eyeless stare finding each other
at the same time between the bed
and the window above the road,
where his basso-voiced sons lifted empty cans
down from the milkstand. Lights were on
in the barn: again he had overslept
because of his eye. He reached it
by stepping back, turned it outward,
thumbed it back in, blinked it into focus,
closed his all-night Bible,
looked out again, his eyes
between curtains his daughter
kept starched and white,
and in his heavy shoulders took the message.

Yarrow

---

you pass through me,
scattering wind inside trees,
softest shudder in the spine
not letting go,

with your damp green fields, small roads,
simplest paths, people stepping out the door

to orchard grass growing
through fallen blossoms
At evening we shook a tree
until the unripe fruit
fell, startling birds,
and they rose together
emptying the sky. Behind the cry
of the birds we heard the moon rise.

Still waters of an early summer,
canals always filled,
and choirs grown large with those who have
returned. You prepare tables.
You know whose children we are
A psalm wanting to speak its love
to those who learned it by heart
but forgot the words, too much expected.

This valley of mountainous shadows,
roses along Stewart Road
red with remembrance, the golden cedar
darker on its other side, splintered edges
of planks across the stream
When an uncle helped me from the stream
because I was drowning, he said
we have our angels, even Yarrow.

The path sliding down to the right,
away from the mountain, a rope silver-knotted
waist high, swinging vacantly
in a melee of stones and grass,
through a tangle of skeletal boy and wire
where the channel shifted years ago
If not overcome by water,
you will live among blue mountains
and green trees. The fields start here,
bending suddenly up
from the water, like young boys at nightfall
finding their clothes in the high grass,
certain they hear voices calling.

Something to catch the sleeves
of those who remember the path to tables
by the stream —
uncertain of their places
and the words of the psalm others begin
in four parts and a descant rising together
like birds to fields beyond.

Janet Kauffman

Janet Kauffman is the author of three novels, three collections of short stories, and three volumes of poetry. She has won a Pushcart Prize twice: once for short fiction and once for her poem "Mennonite Farm Wife." She has been the recipient of a National Endowment for the Arts Fellowship, a Michigan Arts Award, and a Creative Artist Grant from the Michigan Council for the Arts (twice). Since 1995 she has also been doing mixed media work, including handmade books.

Kauffman was born in 1945 in Lancaster County, Pennsylvania, where she grew up on a tobacco farm. After receiving a B.A. in French and English from Juniata College, Kauffman received an M.A. and Ph.D. from the University of Chicago. Currently she is a professor of English and creative writing at Eastern Michigan University, where she has taught since 1988. She is the mother of two sons.

Throughout her life, the work of farming has continued to be important to Kauffman, who has raised hay in Michigan and is now doing wetland restoration. Her poetry collection *The Weather Book* (1981), an Associated Writing Program's Award Series in Poetry selection, focuses on the work and landscape and language of farming. *Where the World Is* (1988) continues her concerns with landscape and the elemental in both the natural world and the human psyche. Kauffman considers herself an "offshoot from Mennonites." Her paternal grandmother and most of her father's family were Mennonite, but her father joined her mother's church, the Evangelical United Brethren (E.U.B.), when they married. Kauffman recalls attending Mennonite Bible school, although she was not raised in the Church. While her poetry and fiction are sprinkled with Mennonite characters, Kauffman, who is known for her experimental style and focus on language, does not concern herself with the realistic portrayal of Mennonite culture. Rather, it has been the alternative viewpoint of the Mennonites, the perspective of cultural critique, that has influenced her.

Mennonite Farm Wife

She hung her laundry in the morning
before light and often in winter
by sunrise the sheets were ice.
They swung all day on the line,
creaking, never a flutter.
At dusk I'd watch her lift each one
like a field, the stretches of white
she carried easily as dream
to the house where she bent and folded
and stacked the flat squares.
I never doubted they thawed
perfectly dry, crisp,
the corners like thorn.

Working Tobacco

1 TOPPING, AS PREFACE

We soaped our hands
with cold soap from a tin can,
then slipped into the rows.
We pulled tobacco suckers, snapped them down,
broke off the pastel flowering tops, with slick fingers
feeling over each plant,
parting the green gumleaves,
steady as prophets who knew how to do things
effortlessly, hands taking charge,
blessing and breaking,
blessing, breaking.

2 STEAMER ON THE SEEDBED

Machines
like mothers pumping the beginning
every April on schedule,
spring steamed

out from under iron,
the metal lids lifting —
and there it was:
great gates opening,
whirring gears and camshafts
winging, the ungainly steamer
shaking wide bull flanks,
shimmering
heatwaves rising through unsteady air,
white clouds bursting into blue
and in the breeze the stinging
water spat off iron.

Somewhere inside the steamer's belly,
roared fire.

3 CULTIVATING

On a two-seated cultivator, we sniffed exhaust,
inhaled blue clouds those long rose evenings;
leaning on a handle in each hand
we weaved around the stalks, furrowing
damp field into dark.
Doubled over and in the drug of it
I watched the velvet plants
with hair leaves moving untouched
below the tractor body, between harrows,
drifting like the blessed on their way.
I let them go.

> *Tobacco's but an Indian weed,*
> *Grows green in the Morn, cut down at Eve . . .*

And now when I see in the shadow of porches
grey farm women nodding
at grey slippered feet,
I feel all over again the curve in my back,
the disproportionate torso
turned like a shell,
the vaginal hold on empty space
and that blue monoxide
cloud of summer we bent beneath to breathe.

4 LEAF

Leaf upon leaf
embroidered on a forest,
gold leaf from green
rib and mesh, elaborate
wind-lifting flags and Caesar's laurels,
miniaturized
forget-me-not leaves in margins,
leave-taking,
palms, pines

simplified to lines —

we draw these
first, a scrawl,
a sign for sure.

5 CUTTING

The tall frame wagons were a rocking
scaffolding on iron wheels.
Tobacco hung like dollar bills,
long and losing green, the thicknesses
of leaf and stalk, gum-hair
plants to lean against, full-length.
In the shed it was the dark hand to hand
swing — catch — swing — catch —
hook of tobacco hanging:
uncle on the rafters overhead,
grandpa over him, straddling air,
father in the black peaked top.
A brown and bitter dust fell down.
The wagons empty, outside,
our cheeks sucked in — it's good —
tasting the grit, the clear
vinegar punch in August in the dry field.

6 VINEGAR PUNCH

Is vinegar and water,
simple to remember as Jesus wept,
with no more sugar than you must,
and nutmeg
you filter through teeth,
sweep with the tongue, spit.

7 SONG FOR HARMONICA

Sir Walter Raleigh is a bust,
a pleasant face upon a sac:

in velvet and opaque pearls
he is a man the girls will say

they lust — they may — knowing well
he's occupied with plots, polite

assassinations, speculative
deals — he's shaking Red Man

hands and taking home the green
leaves, in the hold at sea

curing gold. Who should tell
the story of a pleasant man

with money, paying what he will
for pleasure, and the ruddy girls

and fathers farming for his leisure?

8 TAKING DOWN

A swinging trouble light sweeps through black
barn and cold. My father's breath the fog overhead
caught like a bush in the cone of low beam.
He walks on rails, November nights,
handing down tobacco, long leaves
flattened by the hang and like skins
stretched, veins dry.
We move mechanically under
huge roofed spaces,

among the hammered edges of machines —
tractors, harrows, plows hauled in,
the planter and the flatbed wagons.

Not hunters,
not driven,
we work and do without
the power to cast the shadow of iron,
even as the stun, the hush of arrow over snow —
that speeding dark — comes home.

Round Lake

I tell an easy story, all lies,
at parties. Ask me what I like,
I say digging pits, scrubbing sticks.
Ask me am I married. Easy.
I say no, divorced. You wonder
do I work. Sure, I drill two exact
pinholes in a block of steel.

You I'll tell two things: the summer
I was twelve I saw the rich men from Detroit
without their wives unravel sails
with the care I'd seen them count their cash.
Their hair was white and gray and brushed.
The big sails hooked a wind and then two boats
with even-handed men slipped by,
slipped straight in a hush into blue.
I knew that they were making deals out there.
I thought I'd swim sometime to check
but everybody else said, oh yeah,
they'll hack some waves and yell,
back to your shack, girl. Git, git, git.
But I was sure the men would simply be precise:
Look, we'll tell you this, and this.

I learned to manage pretty well. And next:
when I was seventeen and pregnant, I saw fire
spread across the lake in whorls,
the flames low, swirled, a richness
like embroidery, or golden robes.
I saw this for myself. And again
that winter, looking down through ice
in calms, in paths of blackened fish,
the sparks careened. A few like mica
flecked at the shores of eyes.
The lake steadied itself with lights
every season after.

                   Without leaving home
or reading anything I understood,
I knew what traveling could do.
And here I am with square knots tying lies —
when all along it was the lake,
its blue and white and gold geometry,
that dressy fire, that took me in.

Hunting

At seventeen I should have asked boyfriends
who hunted squirrels and then stewed
spindly legs, to name the barn's colors.
They had clear words for God, but slurred *orchard*,
lisped *death*. I never heard them say *red barn*.
Watching through August nights with them,
I knew the red barns blocked the breeze,
the lights from town; that now the barn was black.
Oh, it was a colorless, lightless world
they walked themselves and gear right through.
There wasn't much to say. We lay for hours
in the heart's holes, in the blown cores
of space, until it seemed like calm
when a wordless hum stopped in the mind.

Betsy Sholl

As an adult Betsy Sholl came into contact with Mennonites through her involvement with several congregations and her husband Doug's pastorate. In 1991 she won the Associated Writing Program's Award Series in Poetry for *The Red Line*. Her most recent volume, *Don't Explain*, won the 1997 Felix Pollack Award from the University of Wisconsin Press. Sholl has taught creative writing at the University of Southern Maine since 1983 and also serves on the M.F.A. faculty at Vermont College.

Born in Lakewood, Ohio, Betsy Neary grew up in Brick Town, New Jersey. In 1967 she received a B.A. from Bucknell University and married John Douglas Sholl. The Sholls have two children. After earning an M.A. from the University of Rochester, Betsy Sholl moved with her family to Boston, where she taught creative writing at M.I.T. for five years and joined the Alice James Book Cooperative, which published her first three volumes: *Changing Faces*, *Appalachian Winter*, and *Rooms Overhead*. She earned an M.F.A. from Vermont College in 1988.

The Sholls were part of a Mennonite congregation in Portland, Maine, for five years while Doug served as interim pastor. In addition, they attended the Pittsburgh Mennonite Fellowship during the spring of 1997. More recently, while serving as a visiting writer at Bucknell University, Betsy Sholl has reconnected with Mennonites through a congregation in Lewisburg, Pennsylvania.

Sholl finds an affinity with the service-orientation and community emphasis of Mennonites. Her own service orientation shows in her work with the Wayside Evening Soup Kitchen, on whose board of directors she served from 1983 to 1997, and in her vigorous involvement in the arts community in Portland. Sholl has been active in the poets in the schools program in both Maine and Virginia. She has also taught in prisons in Maine and Virginia for a number of years.

Soup Kitchen

Ginny at a table of young men belly dancing
their tattoos: gray hair in braids circling her head,
and maybe it's the way they can't make her flinch
that finally soothes them. Maybe the way she
speaks with a *you* that is intimate, gets through
their skulls, and that's why they ask almost sweetly
for rags to clean the mess they've made,

which when I come back is a huge clump of wet napkins
resembling puke and a lot of talk about outer space
inside their heads, with Ginny saying *grow up*,
straight into their guffaws, not like my mother's
clenched teeth hissing that things are hard and it's
not fair, the way we spill our milk night after night.
Out of an old plastic bag she pulls a gull feather

and weaves it though a hole in her sweater.
Evolution, she muses, telling me that down under
the bridge by the ferry, on a hot day she went wading
and saw dragonflies more delicate than any lace
I'm likely to wear, bluer than that blouse over there
across the room. Something planned that, she says,
tapping the vein inside her wrist. She fingers

the embroidery in my blouse, which I got
down the block, used, three bucks, I say, and wonder
if the woman who owned it is here, if she sold it
the way heavier ones sell blood, to wire their veins
hot with liquor. One of the mouthier girls
from two tables away yells — Hey, gimme that shirt.
That's how it is these days, Ginny shakes her head —

as if a little gentleness would kill them. I wonder
through what kinds of gentle and killing she's passed,
under bridges, in train yards. Are there other time zones
where she's had children? But the rule is: don't ask,
don't make her look down and shred her napkin.
Just take what she's willing to give tonight,
which is how she discovered secrets once in a hidden file

her bosses warned her to overlook. They walked toward her.
She could smell the metal of the gun. And then —
she's looking away, fumbling in her purse
for a pair of multicolored mittens she knit by rote
in the darkness of boxcars. She holds them up to the light,
little *x*'s on the thumbs so like my mother's, which she'd
pull out, start over, tightening her lips, while I sat

beside her asking why or what if, till she cried, Stop it,
and my face burned like this old guy Ginny nods to,
who looks plain drunk to me. That too, she says,
but he's got a terrible disease, and across the tables
she calls — God love you, to which he replies with a stiff
bow — Sweet lady, I cry out from my bed every night.
Yes you do, she tells him, and I believe her

since just then field lights come on in the next block
where school boys play soccer. That must be why,
returning her plate to the kitchen for seconds,
I forget I'm not her child. I pick up a piece
of crust pink with lipstick and put it into my mouth,
then stand there in that odd yellow light,
letting it soften.

Autobiography in Third Person

Though she was born late in their lives,
she was not the error her parents feared,
her father's nightmare that she'd emerge
quoting Nietzsche, her mother's worry
that she'd not take to quoting at all.

Still, who doesn't have pages they'd like to
rip from the calendar? For her it is March,
month of freezing rain and downed wires,
Irish moon rising, first ruddy, then blanched,
like her father's bones glaring in the ground.

Deceased, her mother taught her to say,
not *dead*. *Dead* was crude, bones growing
rancid. *Deceased* was a piece of paper,
officially stamped, or a tiny blue spiral
notebook in which she was to record

her moods, then throw them away.
Oh moon heat river paradox running
siren blue uphill as exhaust flakes
rustle down— that was found years later
nearly illegible on her bedside table,

tucked in the marbled notebook where
she re-examines the question obsessing her
juvenilia: Does air, like fog, obscure
the view, blurring color, so one must
choose between clarity and breath?

Does survival depend on distortion,
so the greatest toxin of all is truth?
In that same notebook, recorded
from the last page forward, are dreams.
First, the one where she tries to prod

from the earth a giant stone, the way a pack
of hoodlums would rock a car. But it is huge
and barely grunts, a rancid, pissed off Buddha
bent on breaking impossible desire.
Next, the Mexican beauty parlor, chickens

out front deconstructing the ground. She asks
for color and curls, but the old woman says,
"No, too much — have to choose, choose."
A man with no teeth and a portable phone
is trading in futures. The word *choose*

in different scripts curls through the margins.
Clipped to that page, the draft of a letter,
dated the fourth of March, asks what if
the premise is false, the whole notion of some
reign of error: "Perhaps, Doctor, it's just

a lack of coolant in my veins. What's so sick
about wanting a ghost that doesn't rise
to the surface, mouth some inaudible code,
then slip out of the hands like soap, like
lavender-scented diaphanous soap?"

Don't Explain

I just wanted to tell what I saw —
a brown river, the Raritan, sprinkled
with loosestrife petals, two cassette tapes
dangling from a high bridge, rippled and looping
like kite strings in the wind — but questions came in:
what was the music, snagged on dirty heads,
tossed from a car speeding over the bridge?
And since my father went to school here, could he
have stood at this culvert, stripping petals
into the river? Back then, did flocks of geese
trample the bank down to stark red clay?
Over the phone, Mother says, *Oh sure, sure,*
to the brown water, to loosestrife and geese,
oh sure, the way she'd answer years ago
when I asked, Did they have cars back then? trains?
records? Later there were questions I didn't ask,
darker things — Did you know the same years you were
in school, Billie Holiday was scrubbing floors
in a whorehouse, playing Louis Armstrong
on an old Victrola? That would make Mother wince.
Ditto, if I asked, Were you ever so mad
you could've ripped out your favorite tape
and hurled it, so mad you half understand
the video — Woodstock redux — *Nine Inch Nails*
out-Hendrixing Hendrix, destroying something
they love *and* hate, yanking the keyboard
from its sockets, smashing guitar on amp,
again and again till only the drummer's
left, ducking hurled mikes — God.

I wanted to say wind unraveled those tapes
like an aria too beautiful to be heard,
so we have to imagine the song we'd play
till it wore out, then carry on inside us, wound
on spools of feeling that could spin it to mind any time.
That's what my dead father was to me — on a reel
for my comfort, better than life, till the night
I sat up reading in his own hand, letters
full of slurs, doors he wanted shut against
just about everyone. All night as I read,
my old tape slowed to the indecipherable
rumble of dead batteries and I ripped it out.
Though maybe it snagged on some undergirding
in my mind and still hangs, now limp, now billowing,
inaudible aftermath of rage, small lull
in the music, which lasts a while till something
shakes it up — the way two joggers saw me
on the culvert and just had to shout, *Don't jump,
ha ha.* Balance almost begs for that,
as if whatever made my father so intent
on closing doors, is what makes us now want
to hear the voices that were shut out, want
to rewind and play again the band hurling
instruments and mikes, dumping water buckets
on the crowd dancing in a lumbered frenzy,
young kids lost in the song, whipping their heads
so wet hair stings their faces, feeling part of
the muddy ground, not caring where the crowd
carries them as long as they're moving. And now
the static and screech — is this my father's lost voice
singing inside me, *The world's going down. And down —*
me singing back —*in order to rise?* Down
to where no one's shut out, down to the riverbank's
bare red clay, down to a voice like Holiday's,
that even on a bad tape made from old records,
sends her losses straight to the marrow —*Don't Explain,
Strange Fruit*—voice totally shot by the end,
as if the life couldn't be kept out,
the music couldn't keep itself from breaking.

Redbud

I had to step outside, having just finished
the letters of Keats, who for all his talk of easeful death,
told his friend Brown he wanted to live, wanted his *feeling
for light and shade*, his memories of walking with her —
everything reminds him. *Oh God! God! God!* —
he was barely able to write it, *I should have had her
when I was in health*. Does that mean what it sounds like to us?
Window light and leaf shade on the porch. Next door,
people slipping into their coats, leaving a party. *See ya, Take it easy.*
Hard to believe just last week, I looked up to see a blue truck
crest the hill, flying it seemed, and the driver's surprised eyes
as he fishtailed into me. Barely time to ask, *Am I going to die?*
But nobody did, so can I say it was worth it? say that *beauty*
totaled my car — the stand of redbuds I'd gone to see, purple blossoms
on rain-slick limbs, stark as petals on a painted scroll blooming
above waterfalls, above tiny figures on a foot bridge crossing
a steep gorge. There we were, waiting for a trooper in that fellow's cab,
and it seemed he had to tell how he got caught cheating his boss
at the stables, how he was planning to leave a whole mess
of bad credit, racing stubs, a woman who finally said, *Get out.*
Beauty must have been a kind of charm he knew how to use,
aqua eyes, easy smile, the way he could tell his scam and still run it,
share a thermos, ask ideas for his new name. All around us, those redbuds
so stunning I can't remember now if he drugged a horse,
or fixed a race, dealt off the bottom with his fine jittery hands.
I had Keats in my pocket, himself worried about money,
walking through Scotland to see its waterfalls, astonished
by what he hadn't imagined, the subtleties of tone — moss, rock-weed—
I live in the eye he says to his brother. But they're gone —
Keats, Fanny, Tom, everyone he wrote those exuberant letters to.
What good is *beauty*? Still I saw it, those redbuds, like the moment
making love, into the rush of it, when you think, *I could die now.*
After which — the truck, that fellow telling the trooper flat out
he was doing 50 in a 25, as if beauty has to press its luck,
which the insurance company said had run out:
we'll get him, don't you worry. I don't.
Because he's gone, among the tossing heads of horses,
their nervous sidesteps — gone, without a name,

like those tiny figures dissolving in paint. Imagine,
standing over a gorge where a waterfall plummets — lost,
not so much in thought as its graceful absence, so lost
there is nothing else to want from the world. The *world.*
How beautiful the word sounds. *Whorled.* Purple blossoms
on rain-black trees. The enormous eyes of horses. Rock-weed, slate.
The world loving us, who probably have never loved enough,
never dared let ourselves go that far into its beauty.

Late Psalm

I am hating myself for the last time.
   I'm rolling up angst like a slice of bread,
squishing it into a glob that will rot
   into blue medicine — another joke,
delivered by God, who when you finally
   elbow and nudge to the front of the line,
says, *Oh, but the first shall be last . . .*
I'm considering the roadside grass,
all dressed up and headed straight for the fire.
   "Who isn't?" say the flames,
though it's easy to pretend not to hear
   in this mountain resort with its windows
all finely dressed for the busiest season
   filled with glass fish, turquoise earrings,
infusers that turn weeds into tea.
   "Who isn't poor already?" sing the stalks
of dried milkweed, though it's hard to
   imagine these shoppers in bright ski jackets
coated with road grit, dust from the chunks
   of bituminous coal left outside mines
for the poor to glean. The poor —
   just driving by those bent figures,
filling their plastic bags, here in the 1990s,
   took my breath, made me stop nodding
yeah yeah to the music and pull off the road,
   stunned by the way the years press hard
to fossilize plants, and the poor too,
   who seem to age a month for every

middle-class day. How could they
    possibly hear a blade of grass sigh, "Poor?
There is no such thing." Did I say
    I'm hating myself for the last time?
It's not easy, but I'm loving instead —
    brown teeth, Kool-Aid mustaches, swollen
knuckles, nature's answer to all questions —
    prodigality, those countless insects
and missionary weeds spending themselves
    freely and as far as I can tell, never
rescinding a thing. I'm loving a man
    with his pockets full of pen caps, receipts,
crumpled dollars to put in a beggar's
    dented cup, briefcase bulging with papers,
leftover crusts for the ducks,
    and out of his eyes little fish of light,
glimmering minnows and fingerlings
    leaping between us, flashing
like the tiny carp we watched last night
    in the restaurant tank, appearing through
weeds, miniature castles, a bubbly
    tube resuscitating their atmosphere.
Do they ever conceive of worlds outside
    the only one they've known? Because *he* is,
my man says they're serene, swimming in
    a seamless rippling universe,
not quaking at the sight of monstrous eyes
    leering into the tank, not aching
with the lure of light, lethal burn of air,
    declaring their world a glass prison house.
Rich or poor — who decides? Who wrote
    the stories in which women cry out
all the more when folks tell them to hush,
    and beggars asking for money
get wild rapture instead?

Patrick Friesen

Patrick Friesen was born in Steinbach, Manitoba, in 1946 into a closed and conservative Mennonite community. His native tongue was the Low German spoken by the Russian Mennonite immigrants of his community, but he also learned English early. During his high school years, Friesen rejected the dogma of his Mennonite community, reading Hopkins, Tillich, Spinoza, and Kierkegaard for spiritual sustenance. As soon as he finished high school, Friesen went to Winnipeg, where he received a B.A. from the University of Manitoba. While no longer a practicing Mennonite, Friesen views himself as formed by Mennonite spirituality and culture.

Active in the creation of the arts community in Winnipeg, Friesen served as the founding president of the Manitoba Writer's Guild and has worked both as a writer and editor. Today he is well known for his work in television, theater, film, and video, as well as for his poetry. Recently he has collaborated with dancers and choreographers in the performance of his poetry. His collection *Blasphemer's Wheel: Selected and New Poems* won the McNally Robinson Award for Manitoba Book of the Year in 1994. Since then he has published four more books of poetry: *A Broken Bowl* (1997), short-listed for a Governor General's Award for Poetry; *saint mary at main* (1998), short-listed for the Dorothy Livesay Poetry Award; *carrying the shadow* (1999), and *the breath you take from the lord* (2002), also short-listed for the Dorothy Livesay Poetry Award.

Friesen has described his mother as a formative influence on his desire to write, for she taught him to read before he entered school. His father, however, was a nonverbal man, whom Friesen describes as being distrustful of language. Much of Friesen's early poetry deals with his complex relationship with his father. Friesen has a critical view of the Mennonite community. Nonetheless, he has remained actively connected to the Mennonite literary scene in Canada. Friesen has raised two children and, after many years in Winnipeg, now lives and works in Vancouver, British Columbia.

pa poem 1: firstborn

pa dropped the baby
when he heard it speak
scared as hell to hear the young one talk
thinking of the devil
and the tongue that can take you anywhere

pa confessed the road ahead
his and the boy's
smelled the day of his death   and the child
barely out of diapers
pa glimpsed the future I was going to say
but what he really saw was
the kid on his rear where he fell
with his eyes pinched tight   mouth wide open
and the shadow of the word
that named him dad

pa heard the first word
like headwaters of a flood
tumbling and dark ahead
and pa with his eyes wide
stared at the boy   bare as the day of his birth
and howling with abandon

pa dropped his firstborn
and sat there in the kitchen
alone   and remembering . . .
. . . there was nothing
there

but his sheltered heart
and the saying   da da

pa poem 4: naked and nailed

I remember those carpenter's hands
thick fingers drumming the table
fingers that tightened around my bicep
lifted me right off the kitchen floor
down basement steps
and there we were in front of the furnace
me pleading across your knee   both of us wishing we were
                                                    someplace else
but you not spoiling the child
and you swung that leather high
me twisting to look up   your arm flung out
seeing you naked and nailed like a child to a tree

how could there be so much love?

I wish I could have seen you sidestep
or shout the words of your hurt
even better I would have loved to see you leaping
on your long narrow feet   howling
and sweat flying from that fine muscled chest

what's a father if he doesn't let out
the whirling dervish the gypsy or the juggler?

you one-eyed monster
you saw more than you let on
maybe more than you ever knew
but you couldn't find the words for me

you rowing that boat into mother's dreams
someplace out there   maybe still looking for the words
and one night with me sleeping creepy
you'll find them and you'll find me

sitting in bed shivering
maybe before I find you
you'll tap me on the shoulder
I'll turn
I'll recognize you

and see   you old dead man
how I start with my grievance
and always end up with this Goddamned love
but I tell you that won't happen everytime
or it'll kill me

the moon in the streets

tonight the moon's sunk into the city
and all the houses are shadows
I thought I wanted to break down walls
but I just want to turn from the snow

I want no one's death but my own
the clarity of a struck piano key
the fabric of a plucked string
I want no other life than this

everyone's walking in someone else's shoes
the heart disorders the world
love's mayhem and sorrow drifting
with the moon in the streets

music through an open door
the heat of the room billowing out
I see her dancing on the floor
here at the heart of things

it's st. mary at main
where you forget everything
nothing being born
but the light

clearing poems

2

a slant of light that kind of silver light among the poplars that kind of
    sudden silence
you slow as you approach or it arrives a moment you might have dreamed
    or not
that kind of light stops your breath with fear you stand thin behind the
    last tree
staring at an emptiness filled with spear grass thistles and the end of
    world
so much missing there almost everything you know in the darkness of
    your memory

there is nothing so empty so quiet and becalmed in heat and doldrums
    and shivering at the edge
like the fox or deer you don't enter the field you gaze through the leaves
    and circle
you can't throw your life away you can't enter the abandon you long for
    can you?
a snake slides from a stone pile the hawk's shadow passing and clouds
    wavering in grass
you stalk the lit heart of earth slipping through scrub brush beneath the
    shimmer of leaves

is this disorder this stillness this clearing that shines like an eye this ring
    of bones?
you are a child always you are a child here baffled and waiting for the
    wind
you freeze as if you've been seen you don't breathe all you hear is the
    pulse in your ear
no it is something colder than childhood something unremembered and
    relentless
home ground where you learn to speak in two voices where you are never
    at home

staring clarity the heart diminished to a fist how wind sweeps down from
    a far cold place
there is nothing for this emptiness this moment where nothing is and
    your eyes want to close from seeing

you can still smell the grease of birth on your arms your legs the grease of
   your first birth
and you smell death that old smell of empty places quick as air across
   your face
but you stand looking a faithless man standing his ground at the edge of
   the clearing

4

this is a precise place on your grandfather's farm a hard place by that you
   mean you stumbled on it
and it is hard with stones the brown grass spare and sharp its breath is
   harsh
this place holds nothing else a taut empty womb which birth has long
   abandoned

you surround the clearing with your stealth something more than animal
   something stray
gazing across you see where you were and will be again as you move
   around the world
there is nothing to lose anymore but you don't believe that as your eyes
   search for what is lost

grandfather knew this place it's where he dragged the bones of his dead
   animals
you hear his gruff voice the coarse words that urged the horses in their
   ringing harness
it's a language that wastes neither time nor tenderness but holds what a
   gaunt man knows of love

yes the horses grazed here their brown hides twitching with flies and the
   full smell of their lives
you watched them all afternoon slowly cropping their way to the heart of
   the clearing
standing there coppery in the sun long heads raised to the wind listening
   to you move

and you wonder who hauled their carcasses here later what voice called
   out that afternoon
the farm sinking like a ship into the memory of an old man toothless
   before his god
just the language is left what you learned about words meant beneath
   meaning

and how he strode into the clearing reins in hand turning his horses to
    release the load
how he disappeared again into the trees all lean and bone and calloused
    hands
how his voice faded the air closing behind him and you swung back into
    the silence

15

rain comes down that sparse night rain in october you feel the sad
    rhythm of fall
not sad not quite a whispering among the leaves as if something might
    be alive

your mother playing *träumerei* on the piano and singing you into dream
    with *wiegenlied*
you remember that desire to sing to meet the need in her voice to find
    the words

it's a trap of course there's not a damned thing you can do but reach for
    the notes
what you want is to sing anonymously you want to sing as if you are the
    voice of the world

now you listen to *peace piece* thinking it's rain on the leaves rain inside
    your head
thinking there's not a false note there's no presence outside the playing
    and no player

you imagine his hands hovering over the keyboard anticipation what is
    held back
and what is released his fingers thinking to the bottom of the key what
    can't be sustained

yes it's rain on poplar leaves on a wooden bench rain on a shed's tin roof
    those variations
it's a falling of rain and you're inside it and no it's not his song it's never
    his song

and this touches on what matters doesn't it not how you think about the
    clearing but how you enter
this is about how you live here your mind moving without thought in this
    home

David Waltner-Toews

David Toews was born into a Mennonite family in Winnipeg, Manitoba, in 1948. He attended Mennonite Brethren Collegiate Institute and Goshen College, where he earned a B.A. At Goshen College, Mary Oyer, Mary Bender, and Nick Lindsay were significant teachers in his formation as a poet. In 1971 he married Kathy Waltner and hyphenated his name, and, somewhat later, he became the father of two children. For the next decade and a half, Waltner-Toews pursued training in veterinary medicine (D.M.V., University of Saskatchewan) and earned a Ph.D. in epidemiology at the University of Guelph, where he is now a professor. Much of his research is directed toward integrating socioeconomic, environmental, and health concerns using community-based systems and approaches. His work has taken him as far as Indonesia and Nepal.

Eschewing what he calls "the truncation of consciousness and experience demanded by all modern disciplines and professions," Waltner-Toews brings his interests in science, ecology, and language together in his work as a writer of poetry, stories, and essays. At the center of his creative writing is a passion for community — both the Mennonite community of his ancestry and origins and the global community of which we are all a part. He has published five volumes of poetry, the most recent being *The Fat Lady Struck Dumb* (2001). *The Impossible Uprooting* (1995) features his "Tante Tina" poems written in the dialect-inflected English of previous generations of Mennonite Canadians.

Roots

not about Rudy Wiebe, but for him

Rudy Wiebe, wiping the sweat from his brow,
calls a spade a spade.
He has a spade in his hands.
He is digging a hole near Winnipeg
in the middle of a potato field.
He has blisters on his hands.
He has roots on the brain.
He is looking for his roots.
One foot down he unearths
a nest of potatoes.
Two feet later he has an aching soul
and a sore foot.

His spade has struck a bone.
It is a dry bone.
It gets up and walks around.
Rudy is not sure if it is an ankle bone
or a hip bone.
It may be the bone of a buffalo
dropped by an Indian's arrow or of an Indian
killed by Mennonite good fortune.
Perhaps a Mennonite died here
of overwork and too many potatoes.
Most likely it is the bone of a cow
that choked on a potato.
Rudy Wiebe cannot tell for sure
what kind of bone it is.
He watches the bone walk out to the road
and head toward town.
The people of Winnipeg ignore the bone.
To them, it is just another drunk Indian.

After the bone
Rudy Wiebe takes a lunch break.
He sits beside the hole and eats
rollkuchen with watermelon.
After lunch he continues his search.

There is a lot of dirt in the hole.
There is a lot of dirt in Winnipeg.
The bone gets tired of Winnipeg
and comes back out to the field.
It sits on the nest of potatoes
and watches the top of Rudy's head
going up and down in the hole
between sprays of dirt.

By nightfall Rudy Wiebe
is up to his ears in dirt
but he still hasn't found any roots.
He tilts back his hard hat
shoulders the spade
and trudges home,
bone in hand.
How was your day? asks his mother.
No luck, he says
hanging up his hat.
Maybe you are right.
Maybe my roots are in Russia.

My my, says his mother.
You have enough dirt behind your ears
to grow potatoes.
Rudy pulls a nest of potatoes
out from behind his ear.
Rudy and his widowed mother are very poor.
For supper they have potato soup
with a bone in it.
When I was a girl in Russia,
says Rudy's mother,
we ate this all the time.

A Request from Tante Tina to the Mennonite Women's Missionary Society to Put Salman Rushdie on the Prayer List

Dear sisters in the Lord.
Sometimes when I am the chickens feeding
and the radio by the barn plays,
even like a mother hen the Lord
is me to the kernels of His wisdom guiding.
Many times has the Lord reminded me from
the days in Russia. When the Indians
in Quebec have their guns taken
their graveyard to defend
against a golf course,
I have remembered the Bolsheviks
and how they came to our village
and a factory from the church made.
Ja, but this morning this is not
what I am wanting to say to you.

I have on the radio heard
how the Ayatollah in Iran is wanting
to kill this Salman Rushdie
because he is telling stories
that the Ayatollah doesn't like.
I am thinking then about how John Friesen
has once a letter in Russia written
during the time of Stalin,
and after, how they took him away
just as he the Bible was reading
at the supper table,
and his wife Elsie and the five children
have never seen him again.

Elsie has told me that John the parable
of Jesus was reading about the vineyard
rented to the workers who all the servants
of the owner killed, even the very son,

and then John told how we the earth are renting
from God, and when He comes to ask,
well, how goes it,
what can we say?
And then the kommunists have come
and John has been taken away
and then they have prayed
and then they have schnetki eaten.

And I have told Elsie
that God is in that story,
and how much Jesus is stories loving,
ja, the truth comes to us that way
and we can eat schnetki and life is going on
even then, ja? That is why Stalin and the Ayatollah
and even some Christians
do not like stories so much
because they think maybe God
is in the story hiding like meat in fleisch piroshki,
and when we open the bun
God is on us checking to ask
how we are caring for the beautiful vineyard.

This they do not like,
that maybe God is looking,
and that is why I am asking the church
to put Mr. Rushdie on the missionary prayer list.
As the grain from the leaky pail to the chickens
falls, so can God through Mr. Rushdie
into the world be coming.
And if we the leaky pails are making silent,
then who among us will the Lord's voice be?
Will not even the corn cry out?

Ja, so whenever we are schnetki or fleisch piroshki eating,
let us a prayer for Mr. Rushdie be making.
Here, I have some piroshki gebrought.
Now, let us eat!

How the Earth Loves You

One day, perhaps when you are
in your forties, he is at your door
with a spring of daffodils.
Another day he bears lilies,
or jack-in-the-pulpits,
every day a flutter of fresh petals
and another scent whispering
at the skirt of your hair.
He seems disconcertingly traditional.
He brings roses, for instance, red ones.
You are bemused.
You look past him, sheepishly,
to the shapes of clouds,
to the paling blue sky.
When your eyes return from flight
you see your hand is bleeding,
you are clutching a sprig of thorns,
and he is gone.

He returns with fat red tomatoes,
waxy green peppers, a peach pressed firmly,
gently, from his palm to yours.
You can still feel the scars
from his roses. Your hand retreats.
Your fingers brush.
Your breath like a wave curls under, tumbles,
pulls back. Your belly tenses.
You are body surfing, barely skimming the sand,
an unspeakable fear swelling your tongue.

Do not speak it.
This is what you were made for,
the heat of his gaze on your fore-arm,
burning your cheek.
You feel the slack first in your knees,
then your back. Do not succumb.
The best is still to come.

In the fall, he leaves in a glorious swirl
of gold and rust, amid the chatty travel songs
of migrating birds. You ache in his absence,
raking at the unreachable pain
in your chest. When you think of him,
you balk at his easy certainty,
his knowledge of your desire.
You delight in the melting snow-flakes
that catch in his hair.
You sigh at how his breathing undulates
under the white quilt. It is enough to lie
in bed on a slow Saturday,
to know he will come, his cool palm
stroking your belly, your breasts,
unexpectedly clutching your breath
as if it were another bouquet.

Do not hasten his wooing.
He will come soon enough.
You must not speak his name.
Only when you have slipped life's pearls
through your fingers, like a rosary,
counting the day after day
of his unfailing courtship,
when you have ached for him
in all the little things — in how you walk,
how your fingers probe a place for seeds,
how your cheek presses to his hard belly,
how you touch the mound where new life stirs —
only then will you be ready,
the light will break through
and the darkness, together,
and you will understand, finally,
who it is who has loved you
all this time, so well.

Teilhard de Chardin Surfs the Internet

We speak with voices
neither of men nor angels.
We speak with the ephemeral complexity
of electrons, a conversation
of sand castles, articulating perplexity,
retreating to a sigh of candy wrappers, pop cans,
foam and kelp-litter, scraps of garbage
information, dissimulation,
thoughts for gulls to squabble over.
And as the sea sucks back,
a crab, incredible, unthinking, hard
quotidian experience, a wonder of survival,
scuttles over the traces
of our castles. All over the world,
on the beaches of the internet,
you can hear the hissing intake of breath.
All of evolution's come to this
anticipation, this wondrous
rising wave. For just one cresting second,
in tightening bellies, tumbling over
flashing sand, stars, water, air,
and just before
the flotsam engulfs us,
we shall have spoken everything,
understood
nothing,
the sea will sigh,
and, rising sluggishly heave:
just one more try.

Coyotes at Eyebrow Lake, Saskatchewan

Like a silent, solemn, wire-haired choir,
the coyotes file in
along the coulee's moonlit rim,
awaiting the conductor's whim
to set their voices, held like anxious birds
in slender cages, free.
The poet sinks into the sleepy, self-indulgent
dusk of his tent, unaware.
Eyebrow Lake winks,
flashing a half-moon.
The orgasmic hoot and holler
of the sudden coyote hootenany,
an extended, happy, off-key
full-hearted family campfire song,
breaks over the valley.
The poet scrambles for unidentified
feelings, missing words,
superlatives lost among the musty pile
of socks and two-day underwear.
Sand Hill Cranes lift,
wing on wing, soft, coughing purrs
against the night.
The poet sits, stunned,
amid the litter of his daily rhyme,
terrified by sudden fleeting joy.

Raylene Hinz-Penner

Raylene Hinz was born in 1949 in Liberal, Kansas, to parents who lived in the Oklahoma Panhandle. When she was a year old, her family moved to a dairy farm outside Liberal, where her father "who had dreamed of being a teacher fought the sandy soil and drought to raise an occasional fabulous wheat crop." In the one-room country school where she attended the first seven grades, Hinz-Penner had her first experience as a teacher, helping younger children learn to read. While life on a dairy farm did not permit much travel, a family vacation to Taos, New Mexico, proved formative for Hinz-Penner, who regularly makes pilgrimages to the Taos/Santa Fe area. She has written a sequence of poems about the Georgia O'Keeffe Museum in Santa Fe.

Hinz-Penner came to poetry through teaching. A graduate of Bethel College in North Newton, Kansas, she taught writing and contemporary American literature there for many years, winning the Ralph P. Schrag Distinguished Teaching Award in 1988. Hinz-Penner earned an M.F.A. from Wichita State University in 1995. When her husband, Doug Penner, became president of Bethel College the same year, she took on the position of associate for institutional advancement at the college. Most recently, she has taught poetry to male inmates of maximum security correctional facilities in Lansing and Hutchinson, Kansas. Hinz-Penner has also served as arts editor for *Mennonite Life*, bringing a number of Mennonite writers into print for the first time. Her poems have appeared in *Kansas Quarterly, Cincinnati Poetry Review, Conrad Grebel Review, Sophia,* and *Mennonot,* among other places. She is an active member of Bethel College Mennonite Church in North Newton, Kansas.

Once, in Santa Fe,

when it was my turn to sit beside the old poet,
I watched him eye my fresh work like steaming manure:
What are you doing in Kansas? What does this mean,
he pointed, feigning dazzled confusion.

I had danced with him the night before, a strange
polka no one could follow, and I, too tall to pirouette
beneath his arm like the dark-eyed gypsy of his dreams,
maybe Lithuanian, maybe someone only he could make up,

bored with us and drunk. Today he can't work, his red eyes
oozing as he raises them from my poems. *Get out of Kansas,*
he says. How can I say *it is August, the ditches*
all goldenrod, like the rapeseed fields of China.

— and we too have a history, that century in Russia,
but we were not ones to linger in New York or any lush
valley. Do I sound like my Great-grandfather Ediger's diary?
>   *We bought bread and watermelon in Kansas.*
>   *We met the rest of them.*
>   *At three o'clock we came to Topeka.*
>   *We stayed there three weeks.*
>   *We bought horses and wagons, one cow and iron stove.*
>   *We got on our land.*
>   *We built us a house.*
>   *We plowed five acres up.*
>   *We planted four acres in rye.*
>   *We did much plowing of land.*

I would write for Grandfather a postscript:
>   *We chose carefully.*
>   *More than once. Our hands have held on*
>   *to dreams which bounded from our minds*
>   *as if from a convex mirror*
>   *— when we saw the place, and landed.*

Flowers

I have not missed the irony of this magnetism, my being
drawn to O'Keeffe who posed for hours to display her body
for Stieglitz. In our Kansas home there was no art:
carved wooden plaques or plaster mottoes, *As for me
and my house, we will serve the Lord*; the orange leaves
of a Robert Wood above the rough tan couch; red plastic
carnations in a ceramic vase on the brown metal stove.

No art in school: just Eisenhower's broad catfish grin
beside the flag, the perfect line of ABC cards pinned
to the chalkboard, round-bellied cursives of a tranquil
sameness to pacify us, silent and bent, as we traced
their curled shapes. O'Keeffe loved handwriting, taught her
Amarillo students to address envelopes. We didn't paint,
or study those who did. We didn't wonder

what was in New York. While O'Keeffe developed, black and white,
pulling back her hair to show her skull, arranged her hands
for photographs — the jointed curve of finger, arch of palm —
we curled our hair, our eye lashes, put on layers of scratchy tulle,
turned ourselves into flowers, our skirts tumultuous peonies,
frothing lavender around our thin legs, wobbling pistils and stamens
so fragile and willing, but pointed downward into the ground.

The Opening in Santa Fe

The meaning of a word to me is not as exact as the meaning of a color.
— Georgia O'Keeffe

It is all space, 13,000 square feet, they say,
so you can't see much at once. . . . Did I think

they'd cram O'Keeffe like a Chinese village?
First, the jimson weed, the huge black cross

in a crimson, crimson sky, and Black Place III,
O'Keeffe's voice escaping the dark film room,

ordinary, even, disclaiming. People are slow.
No sidelong New York analysis, just one fervent

argument to convince someone in half-glasses
about "Little House with Flagpole," its arrow perhaps,

free-floating, a weather vane without a pole to hold it,
its nippled blue sun. Mostly silence. Like viewing the body.

The brain can't catch up; language awaits emotion
and there is none. The disconnect. All I can think

is *curve*, and again, *curve*. I try for a brilliant
summation, a response in my guts. I think *curve*.

Line, curve and curled horizon. The artist's desire
a knowing response, deep burst of joy, declamation.

My guilty discovery, that I most enjoy how this show is hung.
Its makeup. The wall, the room's horizon.

How they moved her color through these three, arranged
that series of shapes into five. The white between.

Crossing Over

Some nights,
driving home from anywhere,
I think of that Holdeman woman
who got into her blue car
stripped of its chrome,
her dark hair wound
into a smooth firm knot
under her black cap,
and crossed the line
into the headlights of a truck —
never braking.
Not far from home,
she was not tired.
I see her grip the wheel
against the lure of light.
She will not pull away.

When my mother fretted
over the weave of the suit
my father wore in his coffin,
I only pretended to look.
I could not risk a glimpse
of where his face had gone.

A child will scream, kick
her feet, flail her arms,
reaching for the limit.
I fear that one day I too
will voice a curse in church,
sitting in a third-row pew,
or, as I stand alone to see
the trees, watch the river
rush the deep ravine, one hand
resting on a guard rail,
suddenly throw myself
from a high bridge
into the long fall.

Prayer for the End of the World

Not as they promised us it would be in the Rapture —
two to a plow but only one taken — the other one shaken
but left on soggy earth to watch the bottomsides
of the righteous as they ascend, sucked up to God,
arms skewered, narrow feet dangling.

Let us rather be summoned by geese — the earth aflutter
with the bywinds of their liftoff — drawn from our beds,
our fragmented dreams by myriad flocks feeling their way
to formation, straggling southbound V's. We would come
then, *called*, not running from frantic houses as if
from the first atomic bursts to hide in holes of concrete,
thin sweaters huddled against the wall.

Give us a cool blue dawn. Awaken us with a moon too bright
to bear and the float of heavy bodies as they take the air,
primordial guides true to some sensual knowledge.

Di Brandt

Born in Winkler, Manitoba, in 1952 and raised in the conservative Mennonite community of Reinland, Di Brandt left home for Winnipeg at the age of seventeen. She received a B.A. at the University of Manitoba and went on to earn an M.A. from the University of Toronto and a Ph.D in English literature from the University of Manitoba. In 1987 she published her first book of poetry, *questions i asked my mother*, in which she recalled the experience of growing up within the clearly drawn boundaries of the conservative Mennonite world. The book was awarded the Gerald Lampert Memorial Award and was nominated for the Governor General's Award for Poetry and the Dillons Commonwealth Poetry Prize.

Brandt's second book of poetry, *Agnes in the Sky*, won the McNally Robinson Award for Manitoba Book of the Year. Following publication of her third collection, *mother not mother*, and a 1991 visit to Jerusalem, Brandt wrote *Jerusalem Beloved*. While her earlier works earned her the distinction of being "one of the first women writers to break the public silence of Mennonite women in Canada," the reflections in *Jerusalem Beloved* expanded to include worldwide issues of peace and justice. This book was nominated for the Governor-General's Award for Poetry.

In addition to poetry, Brandt has published a collection of essays called *Dancing Naked: Strategies for Writing across Centuries* and a critical study of maternal narrative in Canadian literature, *Wild Mother Dancing*. She taught English and creative writing at the University of Winnipeg from 1986 to 1995 and now teaches English and creative writing at the University of Windsor. She is the former poetry editor of *Prairie Fire* and a founding member of the feminist editorial collective of *Contemporary Verse II*. Other awards include the 1995 Canadian Authors Association National Poetry Prize and the Silver National Magazine Award for Poetry.

when i was five i thought heaven was located
in the hayloft of our barn the ladder to get
up there was straight & narrow like the Bible
said if you fell off you might land on the
horns of a cow or be smashed on cement the men
in the family could leap up in seconds wielding
pitchforks my mother never even tried for us
children it was hard labour i was the scaredy
i couldn't reach the first rung so i stood at
the bottom & imagined what heaven was like there
was my grandfather with his Santa Claus beard
sitting on a wooden throne among straw bales
never saying a word but smiling & patting us
on the head & handing out bubble gum to those
who were good even though his eyes were half
closed he could see right inside your head so
i squirmed my way to the back of the line &
unwished the little white lie i had told which
i could feel growing grimy up there & tried
not to look at the dark gaping hole where they
shoved out black sinners like me but the best
part was the smell of new pitched hay wafting
about some of it fell to where i stood under
the ladder there were tiny blue flowerets pressed
on dry stems i held them to my nose & breathed
deep sky & sun it was enough heaven for me for
one day

my mother found herself one late summer
afternoon lying in grass under the wild
yellow plum tree jewelled with sunlight
she was forgotten there in spring picking
rhubarb for pie & the children home from
school hungry & her new dress half hemmed
for Sunday the wind & rain made her skin
ruddy like a peach her hair was covered
with wet fallen crab apple blossoms she
didn't know what to do with her so she put
her up in the pantry among glass jars of
jellied fruit she might have stayed there
all winter except we were playing robbers
& the pantry was jail & every caught thief
of us heard her soft moan she made her
escape while we argued over who broke the
pickled watermelon jar scattering cubes
of pale pink flesh in vinegar over the
basement floor my mother didn't mind she
handed us mop & broom smiling & went back
upstairs i think she was listening to
herself in the wind singing

nonresistance, or love Mennonite style

for L. & the others

turn the other cheek when your brother
hits you & your best friend tells fibs
about you & the teacher punishes you
unfairly if someone steals your shirt
give him your coat to boot this will
heap coals of fire on his head & let him
know how greatly superior you are
while he & his cronies dicker & bargain
their way to hell you can hold your

head up that is down humbly knowing
you're bound for the better place where
it gets tricky is when your grandfather
tickles you too hard or your cousins
want to play doctor & your uncle kisses
you too long on the lips & part of you
wants it & the other part knows it's
wrong & you want to run away but you
can't because he's a man like your father
& the secret place inside you feels itchy
& hot & you wonder if this is what hell
feels like & you remember the look on
your mother's face when she makes
herself obey your dad & meanwhile her
body is shouting *No! No!* & he doesn't
even notice & you wish you could stop
being angry all the time but you can't
because God is watching & he sees
everything there isn't any place to let
it out & you understand about love the
lavish sacrifice in it how it will stretch
your woman's belly & heap fire on your
head you understand how love is like
a knife & a daughter is not a son & the
only way you will be saved is by
submitting quietly in your grandfather's
house your flesh smouldering in the
darkened room as you love your enemy
deeply unwillingly & full of shame

the great dark rush of mothering,
the pleasure in it,

the deep need, the suck, the *give,*
give, give, give, give of it.

your hands won't let them go,
you clutch the air

wildly after them — so soon after
they've taken their fill,

slit open your belly, trampled
your sheets,

wanting to be gone.

the colour mothers see most often
is red,

remembering, fiercely, in the
night, tiger's eyes,

firelight, the slight parting of
tall grass, cat's feet,

eyes narrowed into slits, claws
poised, ready to kill:

marauders, intruders, every
dangerous outsider,

the fathers for not being there
when it mattered,

the children's spectacular
hit & run,

themselves in the mirror for
the woman in them,

when what they needed was
warriors, guns,

hand grenades, the whole world
burning.

little one, black angel,
disobedient, wilful,

wild, spirit child.
you wouldn't die.

you wouldn't take
the family lie

into your mouth,
your belly,

the nasty secret,
wouldn't keep it.

naughty one!
wildflower, weed!

flaunting yourself
so flagrantly

between the rows,
the tidy family plot.

you changeling, you!

prancing off into forests,
beautiful green-

eyed faerie,
so very very alive,

coming back,
you miracle child,

you dazzling wonder,
you.

there are no words in me for Gaza, for what i saw
in Gaza, the eyes of the women lining up at the
hospital for milk, with their babies & small
children, their eyes looking at me, another North
American tourist with nothing to offer, except
terrible pity, & shame, shame at my innocence,
my stupid privilege, i never imagined such a place,
i could have been born here, & thought this is what
the world is like, these narrow streets filled with
flies & cowdung, shacks made of sheet metal &
bare wooden boards, the path to the beach littered
with barbed wire & abandoned jeeps, & grey sand,
how long does it take to forget, the soldiers at the
door, the women screaming, the broken china,
embroidered tablecloths flapping in the wind,
blood running from the father's mouth, how long
does it take to forget, the darkness in this woman's
eyes, the children hiding rocks in their hands on
the way to school, these two will not come home
tonight, their shins broken by soldiers in the street,
these eyes, the long long sorrow in them, these
women's eyes, looking at me

Jeff Gundy

Jeffrey Gene Gundy, born in 1952 in Flanagan, Illinois, grew up on his family's farm. He attended Goshen College, where he was introduced to poetry by Nick Lindsay. He continued his studies of literature and creative writing at Indiana University, where he earned a Ph.D. in English. After teaching at Hesston College in Kansas, he moved to Ohio and took a position at Bluffton College, where he has taught ever since. A member of the First Mennonite Church in Bluffton, he is married and has three sons.

In addition to over two hundred poems published in journals such as the *Antioch Review*, *Beloit Poetry Journal*, *Georgia Review*, and *Poetry Northwest*, Gundy has published three books of poems, *Inquiries* (1992), *Flatlands* (1995), and *Rhapsody with Dark Matter* (2000). Gundy has also played an important role in nurturing the new generation of U.S. Mennonite poets and establishing a poetry network. He regularly invites Mennonite writers to read from their work at Bluffton College and sometimes responds to his guests' writings with poems of his own — as in "Where I Grew Up," which uses lines from Janet Kauffman's work as an epigraph. His "How to Write the New Mennonite Poem" includes playfully satiric references to poems by Jean Janzen and Julia Kasdorf.

Although Gundy rarely writes poems on specifically Mennonite subjects, his recent book of prose, *A Community of Memory: My Days with George and Clara* (1996), chronicles the history of his Amish-Mennonite ancestors. He was also the first critic to publish an extensive critical article on the U.S. Mennonite poetry community (see Further Reading). His book of essays, *Scattering Point: The World through a Mennonite Eye*, was published in 2002.

How to Write the New Mennonite Poem

Choose two from old Bibles, humbly beautiful quilts,
Fraktur, and the *Martyr's Mirror* in Dutch.
Get the word "Mennonite" in at least
twice, once in the title, along with zwiebach,
vareniki, borscht, and the farm,
which if possible should be lost now.

Grandmothers are very good, especially
dead grandmothers, especially speaking
German in Russia. They should have
Suffered. Mothers are good and may
have Quirks, if lovable. Male ancestors
are possible but presumed to represent
the patriarchy and to have abused
"their" wives, children, farm animals;
steer clear unless you are Angry,
or can supply affidavits from
everybody who knew them.

It is important to acknowledge
the spiritual and reproductive
superiority of plain coats and
coverings, the marvelous integrity
of those uncorrupted by television
and Mennonite higher education.
Use quaintness, brisk common sense
and a dash of barnyard humor to show
that they are Just Folks Too.

Remember that while the only good Mennonite
is not a dead Mennonite, many dead
Mennonites were really good. Work in
two or three. Dirk Willems
is hot this year. Include a woman,
an African if you know any, and
a Methodist with redeeming qualities.

You, of course, are a backslidden,
overlearned, doubtridden, egodriven

quasibeliever who would be less anxious
and surer of salvation if you could
only manage to give up the car,
the CD player, and coaching soccer.
You really *want* to be like Grandma.
You believe in discipleship, granola,
and the Peace Tax Fund, but things are
Complicated. You think about them plenty.
You plan to give up something, soon.

If you're in a major city, which
you should be, say something about
the streets, how you really hate
the place but get all charged up
walking around on your days off
looking at stuff and drinking
exotic coffee. Mention that this
seems strange to you, as does
the fact that sometimes you like sex,
even when you know the people in
the next apartment are listening.
Put your wedding ring in the poem
to reassure your parents.

Use the laser printer, and send
a large, glossy, black and white
photograph, just in case. Wear
something simple and dark. Smile
but not too hard. Let your eyes
reflect the miles you have come,
the centuries, your gratitude, your guilt.

Inquiry into Gifts, or the Indigo Bunting

After hearing on the radio news
of the beautiful indigo bunting,
of its luminous blue-green splendor
that is visible only with the sun
at your back, I see one that very night
standing calmly on the lawn of a dream.

It knows full well how strange and rare
it is, knows it may live its days out
before anyone sees. As though
the world was made not to be noticed,
as though God had some job for us
besides seeing, as though eyes were given
for making the right turns and keeping
the rows straight. This is romantic,
isn't it? What can I say.
Some dumb gritty pressure,
habit or ideology, is warping me
toward a cautionary space where the birds
are all robins and grackles, beautiful
not even to each other, noisy
and jealous of their turf,
sure that if there is a God
he has done nothing for them lately.
I hear a strange bird call and
look toward the sun and see
a dark shadow, a figure that shakes
itself off to a further branch
before it even hears me looking,
to remind me that what is given in dreams
should not be expected again.

Where I Grew Up

Where the land is flat in all directions, the only relief lies in
gullies. Where the land is flat, ambush doesn't work. It's hard
to die young.
—Janet Kauffman

But every section road is blacktopped now
some with stop signs some without
and with the corn high in the heat
you can see exactly nowhere at the corners.
I used to slow down in the summer
and coast through at thirtyfive or forty
only a little afraid of God and the police.

And so I understand about the three guys
from Gridley who started back a mile
to see how fast they could cross route 24
on a slow Friday early in football season
with the town in a television stupor
a twelve pack of empties in the ditch
a Nova that would do ninetyfive
only wandering a little and the corn
ripping past like half a tunnel.

Flat means something to us here.
There are ways to hide the hill folk
haven't dreamed of yet. The ambush worked
like John Wayne's gun and our boys found
their sweet relief and hard gospel
on the sweaty air and nobody
to argue how many rivers to cross.

Where I grew up the good farmers
have filled and seeded the gullies
into green obedient waterways.
Where I grew up we hate people telling us
how bad we've got it, how deprived.
When we leave we find other plains
or plant crooked rows of green beans
and kill every weed we see.

We teach our children all the stories
of the blizzards and tornadoes,
the droughts and the black deep soil,
its grand slow rolls only idiots
and easterners could call flat —
how we love it, how we hate it,
how it did not quite kill us young.

The Cookie Poem

"Here are my sad cookies"

The sad cookies. The once and future cookies.
The broken sweet cookies. The cookies
of heartbreaking beauty. The stony cookies
of Palestine. The gummy and delicious
olive and honey cookie. The pasty
damp cookie trapped in the child's hand.

Sad cookies, weird cookies, slippery
and dangerous cookies. Brilliant helpless
soiled and torn cookies, feverish and sweaty
cookies. Sullen cookies, sassy cookies,
the cookies of tantrum and the cookie of joy
and the sweet dark cookie of peace.

The faithful cookies of Rotterdam. The wild-eyed
cookie of Muenster. The salty Atlantic cookie.
Cookies in black coats, in coveralls,
in business suits, cookies in bonnets
and coverings and heels, cookies scratching
their heads and their bellies, cookies utterly
and shamelessly naked before the beloved.

Cookies of the Amish division, cookies
of the Wahlerhof, cookies of Zurich and
Strassburg and Volhynia and Chortitza,
Nairobi Djakarta Winnipeg Goshen.
Cookies who hand their children off
to strangers, who admonish their sons
to remember the Lord's Prayer, cookies
who say all right, baptize my children
and then sneak back to the hidden church anyway.
Cookies who cave in utterly. Cookies
who die with their boots on. Cookies
with fists, and with contusions.
The black hearted cookie. The cookie with issues.
Hard cookies, hot cookies, compassionate
conservative cookies, cookies we loathe
and love, cookies lost, fallen, stolen,

crushed, abandoned, shunned. Weary
and heroic cookies, scathingly noted cookies,
flawed cookies who did their best.
Single cookies, queer cookies, cookies of color,
homeless cookie families sleeping in the car,
obsolete cookies broken down on the information
highway. Sad cookies, silent cookies,
loud cookies, loved cookies, your cookies
my cookies our cookies, all cookies
God's cookies, strange sweet hapless cookies
marked each one by the Imago Dei,
oh the Father the Son the Mother the Daughter
and the Holy Ghost all love cookies,
love all cookies, God's mouth is full
of cookies, God chews and swallows and flings
hands wide in joy, the crumbs fly
everywhere, oh God loves us all.

Old Water

---

for Julia and Ginny

If I had known, if I had known, would I ever
have thought to cross the bridge, to
shuck my clothes and slide into the quiet water?
In the fall, leaves languid on the cool lip
as the girls who'd never look at me.
Oh please . . .

When I went under what was waiting
touched me, wrist and thigh, and held firm,
strong, and settled deep with me.
I was desperate, then wild and then
my panic drifted off like an old whiff of skunk
and left the new stars dazzling, scent
of onion grass and violets, the shape below me,
warm and smooth, the body nestled
inside the intimate water.
You could be so free, it whispered.

You could be so good.
I could not speak — and yet
I said, *Not this way.* I said
Not this time. What did I mean?
I could barely think of apples and children,
another life, and then the voice . . . *All right.*
All right. You won't go far.
                              Do I remember
after that? Mud, the hard sticks,
light splayed along the surface. Damp clothes
and my hands among them. Then traffic
and trees and this step, that step, thin
rusty slats of the stairs leading down.

So it's all about God, is it, or else not,
or else it's me and the stream I yearn toward
day and night, hour and year,
the stream I can hear and almost see
as two lovely women swing past
on the other trail.
They do not see me
and I let them go. But oh,
the beautiful saunter
of those women deep in their talk.
They walk the path up the mountain
and the old, old water tumbles down,
tumbles down.

Ancient Themes: The Night

in the dark, where all goes right . . .
— *San Juan de la Cruz*

A morning sweet with bird song and the low grasses
gathering themselves. Two crows on the lawn, the lane
a bit firmer with each dry day. Bench in the sun

at the edge of the winter burn, and a robin clucks
high in the oak grove. I wanted to say that the morning
is sad, that every time is sad, every thing, God

and the sturdy oaks and the oracular missiles
in their cool hidden tubes. Then I wanted to say
that only *now* is sad, its ashy surfaces and lone sheaf

of shivery bluestem. All the rest, before and after,
is something other, muddy and sharp at once,
a shelf of brilliant unread books, the undulant flight

of a cardinal toward its mate. And still the robin
only clucked, and the bluestem shivered, and so I say
what the poet said: The day is joyful, and so is

the dark night. If your love burns bright with yearning,
if you dress in the secret clothes and climb down
the hidden ladder, if you follow the fire in your soul,

then the lover will be waiting in the swaying cedars.

Keith Ratzlaff

Keith Ratzlaff was born in Henderson, Nebraska, in 1953. He attended Bethel College in North Newton, Kansas, where Jean Wedel, his creative writing teacher, and Bob Regier, an artist, became significant mentors in his development as a poet. His first poems were published in *With* magazine, a Mennonite publication for youth, in the 1970s. Ratzlaff went on to pursue his interest in poetry at Indiana University, where he received an M.F.A. in creative writing. Since 1984 Ratzlaff has taught creative writing and American literature at Central College in Pella, Iowa. Ratzlaff has received numerous awards for his writing, among them the Anhinga Poetry Prize in 1996, which included the publication of *Man under a Pear Tree* in 1997. He also won the Theodore Roethke Prize awarded by *Poetry Northwest* in 1996.

Necessity

Something breaks that won't be ignored —
a doorknob, a chair. Today it's the weather
we can't fix, a snow squall
finishing the gradual turning of the trees
by the river. The oaks and mulberry unhinge,
connecting us to the failed things we know.

We would rather watch things stay the same:
the crabapple by the front walk
holding its ground. The apples are useless,
small and hard, but their red is elegant,
so elegant against the white.

We tell ourselves this tree is what we want.
Wherever the snow touches them
the leaves mottle and shine a metallic purple
so unlike the river trees
we almost believe in the newness.

Well, it would be easy to give in.
We could think of our lives as graceful
for having a tree that doesn't drop leaves,
for having wooden apples this winter
to fool birds into coming to the yard.

But half the storm windows need glazing,
the strawberries need mulch.
Somehow it's the trees by the river
that become more beautiful every day.
We don't need the crabapple telling us
not to worry, it's not winter, and nothing dies.
We have to. It is. Things do.

Rough-Cut Head

When the woman in the purple trousers
on the bicycle — now at the corner
now up the street now by the sign
now by the tree — turned the corner,
I thought of her in the dual wind:
the cold one from the west today —
and the other wind beginning with her,
spreading out behind her like geese.
I thought about her flying hair
and the cowl of her skin
and her forehead
defined and reddened by the wind,
of her lips defined and burnished
by the wind. And how even on a bicycle,
how easily we breathe and how easily
our wondrous heads are invaded by the wind.

How open and hollow are the mouth's courtyards,
or the sinuses, or the hallways of the ear.
How vulnerable. How much of us is absence
like drawers, or pictures of absence —
the sky in photos of clouds at night,
the outline of a breast in an x-ray
taken before the mastectomy.
How easy it is to find a place in the skull
for the chisel, or the gun, or the wind
and its glitter. We are alterable.

I know a plastic surgeon who put the gun
in his mouth, fired, and lived.
Think of the echo. The brain in its great hall
banqueting, then besieged. And the joy of impact —
the eyes unbolted, shifting, siting new stars
in the new red sky, the jaw turned to grit
and glitter the wind would fling at us later.
He was depressed for reasons he couldn't name.
In woodshop he has made a letter holder
covered in curious purple spangles.

Gospel

These are our skirts
and these are our trousers
full of us. And these
are our arms in the air
and we are almost dancing.
And these are our grins,
our throats unscrewing their caps,
the pleats of our skirts like ribs,
our feet hovering just
a little way above the floor,
our hands becoming saws,
our voices beginning
to set up the sawhorses
we will set fire to.
This is the boy I was
with a girl on a stage
in a church in Nebraska.
We are leading
the revival singing
for 20 old women
with bony white voices
who will never sing like dogs
for Jesus, howling like us,
but we are indefatigable.
We are trying to
set fire to the walls
and singing Oo,Oo,Oh,Oh Lord
from the absolute red wells
of our throats — I'm singing
like the day I fell out the car window,
the first day my body discovered
its real predicament
and sent my voice out for help;
and she's singing like the day
she found Jesus
which was the trouble.
I was perfectly, shamelessly

in love and lying and doing my best.
But nothing I hoped for happened.
Either there in the church
or with her, later.
All that misdirection
and shame. Not even half
of what I've ever wanted
has risen up singing
like an impudent animal.

Group Portrait with Ukuleles

Once I was a boy
in a classroom
of boys learning to play

the ukulele. In the end, even
the stumpfingered
learned three chords:

G, C, D7. Our big felt picks,
our whiny
little strings. We were a part

of the American Folksong
Revival
in spite of ourselves,

in spite of our penises
and voices
rising and falling like elevators.

Imagine us, our 25 faces
still forming,
heads slightly out of round,

singing "I Gave My Love
A Cherry,"
or "Big Rock Candy Mountain."

There was the recital
we never gave
because, to tell the truth,

we weren't very good.
One boy is dead
now, three are welders,

two joined the Navy, one
sells used cars,
half a dozen are farmers,

one has been convicted
of exporting
Nazi literature to Germany.

I don't remember any of us
as mortal
or talented or cruel.

All we ever learned was that
chord progression,
knowable and sequential —

beautiful as gears shifting —
something useful
and at the bottom of all

the music we imagined we
could care about.
We knew who Mozart was

but there wasn't any Mozart
for the ukulele.
That would have been wrong

and we knew it — some of us.
Or none
of us. Either way.

My Students against the Cemetery Pines

are writing poems about death and resurrection.
That's the assignment — to handle death
as an artistic problem. We've worked on it.
Last week Ruby brought the husk of a bird
she'd found on the street to class,
so we put it on a pedestal and wrote
still lives. We've studied Caravaggio's
The Entombment of Christ and have written
poems based on the structure of lamentation,
poems poised with both hands in the air
or hands lowered or hands fallen. Today
I showed them doom paintings — the massed dead
rising from battlefields and barracks,
from the New Jerusalem, from prairies, the sea.
I told them there was a lesson there for poets.
In not one of them, I said, do the dead
have any time for anything else — not the world,
not us in these corrupted bodies.

And if the dead rose up now,
whole and effervescent from under their stones —
the four drowned Koslovski children
in their muddy shoes, my neighbor who died
with five years of newspapers waiting for the paper drive —
I doubt my students would blink. They would write poems
in all seriousness because that is what I've taught them:
It's what you do with death and its extensions.

So this is the assignment:
there must be water, there must be light
of some kind, there must be a bird in the poem.
Stanza one must be written looking out over the water.
It's March and the ice is shoaled up in waves on the shore;
a flock of shovelers has landed in the circle
of open water in the middle of the lake.
To write the second stanza, I say, don't turn around.
Feel the graves behind you, the pines and
the ecstatic structure of the dark boughs,
let something rise up immortal and with hands.

And when suddenly the literal dead do rise up,
my students' backs are turned. They are looking
at the water, inventing dark birds and nuns
married to Christ. And the dead rise up
with no dirt in their mouths, with clean shoes
and crystal voices singing "This is it! This is it!"
And I tell my students to stay focused,
to wait for it. Stop. Don't turn around.
Say no it isn't, I tell them. No, No, No, No.
The first line of stanza three is "No it isn't."

Dill

This is my mother's last garden
before she moves from her house.
The apartments from now on
grow small and then smaller
until finally she will live
in just her body and then
not even there. It's not tragic,
but there's heaviness, grief's
first cousin, in the air.

The garden's small:
two tomatoes, one cucumber,
some transplanted pansies.
The iris need lifting but
she'll leave that for someone else.
Whoever, she says. The rest
is ruin she's left to volunteers —
purple larkspur and the yellowish
proto-flowers of dill — so much dill
risen up it's been transformed
from herb to uselessness to beauty.

We all know where this is headed.
The great forces are playing
all around us — light, inertia,
time, gravity holding us down

like the bully it is. Then the fist,
the boot, the years, the corn knife
we'll take to the larkspur, its
purple candles, its tall sorrow;
to the dill —*anethum graveolens*—
named for its heavy smell,
its relationship to grave and gravid,
to son and aunt, brother and daughter,
to strife and harm and weight.
This isn't a lament. Okay, it is.

Ann Hostetler

Ann Elizabeth Hostetler, born in Mount Pleasant, Pennsylvania, in 1954, spent the first years of her life in Scottdale, Pennsylvania, home of the Mennonite publishing house, Herald Press, where her mother worked as an editor and book designer. The oldest of three children and the daughter of two writers, Hostetler grew up surrounded by books. When she was eight her family moved to Edmonton, Alberta, for three years, where her anthropologist father taught at the University of Alberta and researched the Hutterites. The family made numerous trips between the eastern United States and western Canada as her father pursued his research in communitarian religious groups. As an adult, her own research interests in multicultural literature have led her full circle to an examination of the Mennonite faith and culture into which she was born.

After Hostetler earned a B.A. in art from Kenyon College, she worked in publishing for several years in New York before returning to graduate school to study literature. She received an M.A. in English from Pennsylvania State University and a Ph.D. from the University of Pennsylvania. During this time she also married Merv Smucker, with whom she has raised four children. The family settled in Milwaukee, Wisconsin, where Hostetler taught at Marquette University, the University of Wisconsin-Milwaukee, and the University School of Milwaukee. She has received a Wisconsin Arts Board Development grant. Since 1998 Hostetler has taught English and creative writing at Goshen College. Her poems have appeared in the *American Scholar*, *Cream City Review*, *Mid-America Poetry Review*, *Mothering*, the *Mennonite*, and other places. Her first volume of poetry, *Empty Room with Light*, was published in 2002.

Painting with My Daughter

We wet the dry discs,
soak the brushes in ultra tones —
royal blue,
magenta, aquamarine —
wisps of brush stroking
mark the thick paper,
the silence,
faint inrush of breath
when the world runs together
making volcanoes of color
in the early shadows of November afternoon.

After we finish
I stand before the window
flushing out the pigments
at the kitchen sink,
red and blue bleeding from the brushes
into the stream of clear water.
I hear her singing to herself
in the next room,
already caught up
in something new.

I do not turn on the light
but stand as shadow thickens
objects around me,
the window before me a square of fading light,
framing bare branches,
a frozen garden,
the cracked blue plastic swimming pool
from last summer.

Iconoclast

My grandfather Ezra painted a gigantic face
on the side of the shed when he cleaned his brushes,
stroking the weathered boards with leftover barn red,
till a man with worldly mustache and pompadour

stared out across his half-section of Alberta wheat.
Ezra himself kept the Ordnung, shaved his mustache
and trimmed his beard, though he played baseball
on Saturdays. Nothing wrong with a little fun.

But a newcomer moved in down the road,
complained that his neighbor had painted a pinko
for everyone to see. Ezra shrugged, whitewashed the shed,
returned to the plow with a book in his hand.

No matter if the furrows are crooked, he said,
the seed will sprout just the same.
And Sundays after church he drew eagles
in the margins of his Bible.

Female Ancestor

for Irene, whom I never met

A farm woman opens
the oven door of the coal stove
to stir the embers, re-latches
the door with a cast iron tool, sets
it down, wipes her hands, moves
to the sink where she bends
to peel and soak potatoes. She turns
to wipe down the oil cloth,
unbottle pickled beets
into the blue glass dish passed down
from her grandmother.
After the meal she bends over
the sink, scrapes and washes

crusted pots, feeds scraps
to the dog. Her daughter dries
and puts the dishes away.

For decades the woman bends
over washing, over mending.
She hangs out the heavy sheets,
bends over ironing, over tubs
of water drawn from the cistern
and heated for baths.
She bends with sleepy children
over their school books,
bends over their fever-flushed
faces. Twice she bends over
a tiny coffin. She bends
over her husband's back,
her veined, callused hands
kneading his work-hardened
muscles. Before she dies
she cuts down one of his suits
to make a traveling outfit for her daughter,
and hums as she bends over her sewing,
thinking of the long train ride to college
that will take her daughter away
from the farm forever.

Resisting Geometry

The first time I saw my father defeated
he was leaving the only parent-teacher conference
he ever had concerning my academic failure,
his black raincoat drooping over one arm.
Settling his other arm over my shoulder,
he walked me to the car, told me about
his sixth-grade failure to master fractions.

How could I explain to him
it was the axioms themselves
I objected to, knowing that, like his whims,

I had to take them on faith.
Tested against experience
they appeared to be correct —
no two points could occupy the same space
at the same time; lines perfectly parallel
will never intersect; a straight line
is the shortest distance between two points.
But such self-evidence troubled me.

Imagining exceptions, I felt called
to test the axioms, to wage a battle
against givens, resisting at the root.
When the boy circled Mr. Oelkers
at the blackboard, arguing logic,
I sat at the back of the room
drawing shapes that defied these laws.

It was only in the spring, sprawled out
in front of the stereo, listening to James Taylor
and embroidering the margins of my geometry book
with blue ball-point pen, that I discovered
what was at stake for me was the axiomatic quality
of reasoning itself, the ways in which our assumptions
construct reality, become paradigms
that organize our vision.

I realized that no one else took geometry
as seriously as I did — at least no one
who was failing, that is — and that
in order to get on with life
I would have to get beyond axioms,
memorize theorems, prove hypotheses.

This was not art, where my doodles
might have some eccentric meaning.
This was a game with rules
and if I put aside my distrust of logic
long enough, I could learn to play.
But there was no longer time
to be good at it, only time to garner
a hard-won D.

When the final report came home
I tried to explain my triumph to my father —
my passing as an act of will —
that at the last minute
I had mastered something more
than grades reflected. As I began
to speak a shadow settled over his face.
Even at fourteen I saw that he was weighing
how much he could take on faith.

Priestess of Love

I wanted to be a priestess of love,
angel of mercy, crystal in a sun-streaked window
staining the world, a dark red valentine pressed
between the pages of a schoolboy's book, an obscure
poem about water, wind, stone, heat
of sun on rock, a musk-scented grove of fern.
Instead I drew psychedelic patterns
on my toes with colored marker and flaunted
them through my leather thongs
at my best friend's older brother
when he took us in his yellow Mustang to hear the burning
cool flute of Herbie Mann. I wanted
to cover myself with paint and roll on canvas,
make art with the instrument I loved the best,
my virginal body with its swelling breasts,
twin pelvic bones delicately protruding on either side
of my barely risen belly. Like the moist,
searching tongue of a deer stripping bark
from a sapling I thirsted for the world,
like tiny bubbles in champagne
I rose and crested,
waiting to overflow.

Juanita Brunk

Juanita Brunk was born in 1955 in Newport News, Virginia. After attending Eastern Mennonite High School, she spent several years at Eastern Mennonite University before completing her undergraduate degree at James Madison University. She received an M.F.A. from George Mason University. The first recipient of the Creative Writing Fellowship at the University of Wisconsin-Madison, Brunk has also taught English as a second language and writing classes in Pennsylvania; Washington, D.C.; and New York. In 1996 Philip Levine selected her first volume of poetry, *Brief Landing on the Earth's Surface*, for the Brittingham Prize from the University of Wisconsin Press. She also received the Great Lakes Colleges Association New Writer's Award for this volume. Her work has appeared in the *American Poetry Review*, *Passages North*, *Cimarron Review*, *Southern Poetry Review*, and *Poet Lore*.

Although Brunk is not a practicing Mennonite today, the layered images of family in her poems about the past reveal the context of the Mennonite community as one of their multiple layers. Brunk does not write as a Mennonite, but the Mennonite context she grew up in is subtly implied in the complex tissue of memory these poems re-create. Her poems celebrate the body and the primacy of the senses as a way of knowing the world. At the same time, they are elegies to the body's impermanence, ranging from explorations of self-love and self-knowing, as in "On This Earth," to affirmations of eros. Brunk lives in New York with her husband and son.

On This Earth

To love my own, my body,
to know without saying, *legs, you are good legs,*
and feet and stomach and arms, good, and the spaces
under my arms, and the brown pigments
splashed across my back like tea leaves.
To love my body the way
I sometimes love a stranger's: a woman
on the subway, tired, holding her two bags,
a child slumped against her like another sack
as the train stops and starts and the child says something
so quietly no one else can hear it,
but she leans down, and whispers back,
and the child curls closer. I would love my body
the way a mother can love her child, or the way
a child will love anyone
who gives it a home on this earth, a place
without which it would be nothing, a dry branch
at the window of a lit room.

Letter to Myself as a Child

You wake to birdcalls,
your mother's footsteps down the hallway
past your door. *Amazing grace,*
she sings, her arms piled high with laundry.
Sunlight warms your face
and dawdles in the sheets. You rise, dress,
leave the house as if on urgent business.
Barefoot, you leap across high grasses
in the field, drag the dinghy through mud,
throw in a life preserver
that you never wear
and row south, past the duck blinds
and buoys that mean *deep water,*
past the sandbar.

The house is small in the landscape.
As though you were already gone, you dream a little
of your life there, but what you think of mostly
is the way this river leads into a larger river,
bay, then ocean. The sun beats down
on your skin, warm and brown,
and you lift the oars
into the hull
and lay a palm against your belly,
stroke your thigh. *Amazing grace,*
deep water. The tide turns
your drifting boat toward the river's mouth
and, further, toward a flickering spot of white,
so tiny and uncertain
it's barely more than premonition,
a gull's wing or a sail
reflecting light.

My Father's Tongue

My father could not say the words.
They were heavy as bricks or lumber;
they took the shape of stairways, scaffolding,
buckets of stucco or concrete.
They multiplied,
became buildings with rooms and puttied windows,
walls braced and sheathed to hold in heat
or hold a whisper out, doors
that could be slammed.
They were the clothing strangers left
in a ditch, reeking and stiff, crusty trousers
that he found and carried home in cardboard boxes,
rank woolen jackets waterlogged
with mud and soot,
heavy coats that shrank
in the washer and shed chunks
of gritty lining in our clean socks and underwear.
They were the neighbors' discarded appliances

salvaged on trash day and piled up
in our basement to be fixed:
hair dryers with melted innards, doll carriages
without wheels, lamps with frazzled cords
and dangling necks.
The things my father couldn't tell us
were cars that stuttered and broke down
by the side of the road,
nothing to do but stop
and see if you can make it right,
his hands with wrench or crowbar or hammer
battered from trying to make us hear,
one thumbnail always bruised
or growing back.

All Sweet Things, Like Forgiveness, Are a Falling

Think of cushions on a sofa
in the house where you lived as a child.
Evenings when you settled there your head grew heavy,
dropped, and you left behind the grievances
and clutter of the day, let your arms
and legs go slack and undemanding,
losing will. You drifted
from your body, from the room
with its cumbersome chairs like sentries
and lamps that puddled light onto the dark creases
of your father's face and onto your mother's hair
where she sat, sewing. How simply you fell,
spiraling gracefully downward
into shifting territories
of light and undiscovered languages
you understood. And if you woke or half-woke
later, you heard the clink of dishes as someone set the table
for tomorrow's breakfast, your own milk mug
at your place. A distant pulse,
the household carried on
as you were lifted, carried;

voices —*the window, Ruth*— sheets drawn
around you, a lamp clicked off.
All sweet things happen
in that place where, once more, you are falling,
holding nothing, holding nothing back. In a far province
a tailor catches light on his needle
and weaves it into clothes that you will wear.
Bells are being cast to wake you.
A feast. A land peopled
with strange faces you will grow to love.

Where My Mother Cries

It is always November, the driveway lined with gold,
the air rich with the smell of burning leaves.
Other years she placed the brightest leaves in silver bowls
with evergreens and mums; the house
was sweet with autumn. In order not to ruin
a picture I've made for her at school, a woman

and a girl, I walk carefully. The woman
is tall, her hair a fury of gold.
The two are smiling in the face of ruin:
trees with black leaves,
a burning house,
smoke drifting in a capsized bowl

of sky. I know the sky is not really a bowl.
It goes on forever, like time, that will change me to a woman,
claiming everything. I enter the dark house.
In the kitchen, a row of pots gleams gold
against the wall. I leave
my jacket on a hook, neatly, as if ruin

did not live here, as if ruin
were not a dark bowl
my mother has fallen into, and will not leave.
She seems like someone else, another woman
with her skin, her eyes, her brown hair shot with gold
and gray. She is not at home in this house

though she sits in the house
all day in a ruin
of yarn, knits a scarf the muddy gold
of mustard, grows thin, will not eat from the bowls
of soup my father offers. Once a woman
begins to leave

she might leave
everything, her house,
her children. Once the woman
recognizes ruin,
it might be everywhere, in someone's hands, or in a bowl
of soup, the rich broth yellow as fool's gold.

Where my mother cries, a woman gathers autumn leaves.
They look like gold, or summer's ruin.
The silver bowls are mine. There is no house.

Papaya: Lancaster County

Inside the Amish health food store
Mattie, the eldest daughter, stuffs wedges
of papaya into plastic bags and fastens them
with rubber bands, the thick brown braids
of her hair tied back
beneath a bonnet. I think about papaya,
swinging in fat globes on the trees of a country
she'll never visit, being harvested by people
she might struggle to imagine,
and of the way it's sliced
and dried and shipped
across an ocean to end up
in her hands in this dim store
where a wooden sign says
Miller's Food. Horse Ties in Back. No Photography, Please;
and the clocks are never changed to daylight saving.
It's early, only seven-thirty, standard time.
Later, tourists will come
with cameras and brochures

and photograph her weighing onions,
slicing cheese. But now, her face inscrutable
and calm, she moves among shelves of almonds and pine nuts,
herbal teas and remedies that reek of hay.
She nods, but we don't speak.
We're strangers, really.
I know nothing
of what she does or doesn't long for.
If we meet at all it's through the dumb heaviness
of fruit, lifted from palm to palm,
our fingerprints joining in the bright flesh
of the papaya, the puckered skin of the prune.

Shari Miller Wagner

Shari Miller was born into a Mennonite family in Goshen, Indiana, in 1958 and spent time in East Africa (Kenya and Somalia) during her formative years when her physician father was on assignment there with the Eastern Mennonite Board of Missions. She received a B.A. from Goshen College and an M.F.A. in creative writing from Indiana University, where she studied with Yusef Komunyakaa, Maura Stanton, Scott Russell Sanders, and Roger Mitchell. Nick Lindsay, who taught poetry writing at Goshen College, was also an important teacher who "emphasized the importance of having a poetic vision — and of taking responsibility for that vision." Wagner's interest in travel and service has taken her to Haiti and Honduras and led her to take a two-year service assignment with the Mennonite Central Committee at a Choctaw reservation in Louisiana, where she collected oral histories. She has taught writing at several universities and at a Cherokee reservation in North Carolina, has conducted writing workshops in nursing homes and elementary schools, and is the editor of *MennoExpressions*, a publication of the First Mennonite Church of Indianapolis. She is married and the mother of two daughters.

Wagner has received both a Master Artist Fellowship and an Associate Artist Fellowship from the Indiana Arts Commission, as well as two Artist Fellowships from the Arts Council of Indianapolis. She has received Poetry in Motion Awards for her poems that appeared on public buses. Her poems have been published in the *Southern Poetry Review*, *Indiana Review*, *Black Warrior Review*, *Midland Review*, *Artful Dodge*, the *Mennonite*, and the *Mennonite Weekly Review*. Recently she has been traveling to "sacred places" in Indiana and writing poems about them; one of these poems is "The Sunken Gardens." She has also completed a poem cycle about the Hochstetler massacre, which occurred in the mid eighteenth century in Pennsylvania.

A Cappella

As we gasp between lines
a chasm opens
from the older hymns.

I sense a darkness
like what I heard
at an Amish barn door,

the entrance to a church
or a cavern
where my ancestors

droned the poetry
that could not be uttered
in the village.

In sixteenth-century
dungeons
they sang these hymns

as a way to connect
flesh chained to walls
and racks. We hold

these broken ones
in our voices
like bread that could

bless us. Grandma Mishler,
whom we buried
the Easter when hyacinths

bloomed inside ice, leans
behind my left shoulder
and Shawn with the quick

laugh who died
giving birth
sits beside Grandfather

on the couch. They listen
with their eyes closed.
All of the old ones

are here in the dark
room of a house that
stood where corn grew

because God sent
the sun. We end with
"Praise God From Whom

All Blessings Flow"—
the version with echoing
alleluias and amens.

We don't need the book
and no one sets the pitch.
We've sung this one

at every marriage
and funeral. Even in-laws
with eyes on the last

five minutes of a game
join in from their corner.
From every direction

there are voices within
voices, husks beneath
husks. The dead sing

in a house so haunted
we breathe
the same breath.

Rook

The rook was the first
bird I recognized. Garbed
in black, it resembled
my great-grandmother who
warned against vanity
and the worldliness of face
cards with their kings, queens,
and jacks. Good Mennonites

chose rook instead of pinochle
or poker. Perched upon
a lap, I learned my colors
from the cards and pondered
the ambiguity of words —
how someone could lose
a hand or look inside a kitty.
My father could con you
into going set with his
physician's face but my mother
and her family of farmers
would forecast their failures.
"Oh, gussy," Aunt Doris would
groan. "I don't have anything
above a twelve." Even
their battered cards revealed
where the bird had come
to roost. When I turned thirteen,
we packed the deck and moved
to the Horn of Africa where
missionaries hunched around
kerosene lanterns to play
rook low with a double deck.
I could sense concentric circles
surrounding our table —
the compound, the village,
the desert, the ocean.
The encyclopedia said our bird
was omnivorous like marabou
storks, those stately old
gentlemen who stood statuesque
in the garden but in a lunatic rush
devoured left-over scraps. Back
in Indiana, the game for pacifists
became a war between the sexes.
Young men began the bid
at 140 and dared to shoot
the moon while their opponents
watched each other's faces
to deduce when to "check"
or "pass" and which trump

SHARI MILLER WAGNER (119)

to call. Normally, I couldn't
speak to boys, but at my cousin's
church parties, as I arranged
my fan of cards, the bird
whispered the words to say.
Years later, my fiancé taught me
poker and I schooled him
in the rudiments of rook before
introducing him to my parents.
He found it strange that when
the dead hand was my partner
the bird would nest inside
the stack and when we traveled
rooks seemed to follow us
like Woden's ravens, Memory
and Thought. When Grandpa forgot
the trump color and values
of cards, we substituted Uno
until Alzheimer's stole even
that away. Since then, we keep
our decks inside a drawer.
The men stretch out to watch
sports on cable while women
congregate in the kitchen to talk
about children and exchange
photographs. Our new games
are always changing and it takes
time just to learn the rules.
Last Christmas at Doris' house,
we shook tiny pigs whose flanks
we read like dice and on my
father's side we played a game
of '60's music with lyrics only
my husband knew. As my uncle
ruminated upon the second line
of "Suspicious Minds," our blackbird
scratched his angry talons
against the box of Trivial Pursuit.

Second Language

On their ankles and arms girls wore
leather bracelets with oily lockets
sewn shut like their virginity.
My father who took out stitches said
they carried them for a charm to ward off
demons and disease, serpents that slept
in the same fields. You would find
if you cut them open, pages from
a holy book with print too small to read.
I wondered how they knew the words
were in there. This was the year

I turned thirteen, began pecking out
poetry on a manual typewriter with sticky
keys that left smudges around the letters.
I wanted to describe large, empty spaces,
the desert where Somali nomads carried
their houses. As they walked they composed
in an unwritten language lyrics
that traveled in circles like the wind
or the voice of the young muezzin
calling from the minaret of the mosque.
Even in my bedroom his notes rippled
through darkness growing larger.

I never leaned the language, but
later rustling corn leaves spoke
a tongue I hadn't heard before and carved
deep in the skin of beech were cryptic
poems I could partially decipher,
words of love or loss we carry
within us, our amulets, our houses,
as we travel through desolate spaces.

The Sunken Gardens (Huntington, IN)

For my grandparents, Perry and Lucile Miller

Winding paths lead near cool waters
and masses of bloom, in the place made out
of a dream.
—Better Homes and Gardens, *Nov. 1929*

Poised on this limestone bridge, grey now,
but then it shone white, Lucile still wears
her bridal corsage, orchids pinned
to a stiff tailored suit. They have come,
like the others, to gaze into the cathedral
of their melded shadows where goldfish,
like shards of stained glass, glide. They marvel
at such beds of begonias and swirling
iris bordered by coleus. If paradise
can be designed from the raw gape
of a quarry, then the years can only add
their layers of bloom — cascading roses on Time's
great trellis. For the moment, at least,
they cannot foresee how this radiance
will fade, how negligence will mow
the flowers and vandals seize the rest.
Stone, water, grass . . . that's all
that will remain, the bare geometry
of a garden when memory has eroded its own
lush bank and they can't see beyond
the retaining wall somewhere in the thickening
mist, petunias so white they ache

in the moonlight. This pool has no bottom
but mud and more mud, but that can't be true,
and though you both wander through mazes
of beige hallways and can't reach each other
somewhere there must be a place, a chapel
freshly green where you meet. Maybe

it's here—on this bridge—where traffic is muffled
by maple leaves miles above what matters
in a life immortalized by the sudden
brush of a kiss.

Sheri Hostetler

Sheri Hostetler has been well known among Mennonite (and not so Men-nonite) writers as the founding editor of *Mennonot: A Journal for Mennos on the Margins*, an alternative magazine she published from 1992 to 1999. *Mennonot* provided a much-needed outlet for poetry, critique, humor, and dia-logue among those connected to, but not always in the mainstream of, the Mennonite community. Unique among Mennonite publications because of its noninstitutional character, *Mennonot* was truly, as Hostetler says, "a pub-lic forum in which to speak honestly."

Sheri Hostetler was born in 1962 in Millersburg, Ohio, and spent her first twenty-two years in the state. She received a B.A. in communications from Bluffton College and spent a year studying journalism at the Univer-sity of Missouri-Columbia before earning an M.A. in theology from the Episcopal Divinity School and studying at the Pacific School of Religion, where she received the Clare Fischer Feminist Scholar Essay Award from the Center for Women and Religion. Hostetler began writing poetry when she was twenty-eight, and her poetry has appeared in *13th Moon, Creation, Sojourner: A Woman's Forum, Mennonite Life, Paterson Literary Review, Ruah,* and *The Writing on the Wall.* In the fall of 2000 Hostetler became the pastor of the First Mennonite Church in San Francisco.

Not of This World

I am like none of you. You must recognize
deep in me how different I am. You're all
Wonder Bread and drive-ins. I am fertile
fields, head coverings, memories of martyrdom
like yesterday, hymns without organ. The
Bible whispers in my ear at night, it will
not keep still.

But my people do. *Die Stille em Lande.* We
never talk. Quietly we move, quietly the
fields are plowed, in quiet are the dishes
washed, the sheets pulled taut, silently the
hay flung high atop the wagons. Our horses
clip clop in a virtual vacuum. All around
us pins drop, and, still, we are still.

Nature loves our vacuum, blesses us with a
bounty you cannot imagine. Look at our barns,
they are filled with sweet hay, hay without
end, stacked fragrant, stacked sweet. We
do not talk but we smell the sweetness of
hay everyday, oh stranger, you know not what
you are not.

I am not like you. I talk with you, laugh
with you, make love with you, break bread
with you, I will even die with you. And my soul
will rest atop a haymow on Weaver Ridge while yours
goes to heaven.

Say Yes Quickly

Say yes quickly, before you think too hard
or the soles of your feet give out.
Say yes before you see the to-do list.
Saying maybe will only get you to the door,
but never past it.
Say yes before the dove departs for, yes,
she will depart and you will be left
alone with your yes,
your affirmation of what you
couldn't possibly know was coming.
Keep saying yes.
You might as well.
You're here in this wide space now,
no walls and certainly not a roof.
The door was always an illusion.

Instructions

Give up the world; give up self; finally, give up God.
Find god in rhododendrons and rocks,
passers-by, your cat.
Pare your beliefs, your Absolutes.
Make it simple; make it clean.
No carry-on luggage allowed.
Examine all you have
with a loving and critical eye, then
throw away some more.
Repeat. Repeat.
Keep this and only this:
    what your heart beats loudly for
    what feels heavy and full in your gut.
There will only be one or two
things you will keep,
and they will fit lightly
in your pocket.

The Woman with the Screw in Her Mouth Speaks

When people are starving, they go inside. This is the only way
to survive. Conserve. Save. Go to the quiet place in yourself
and wait for the day food comes. Wait without hoping,
for hope takes energy and you have very little to spare.

We went inside, too, but we wrapped our silence around a kernel
of fear. This fear fed us, and for this we were grateful. It made us
shrewd and cautious, not dim-witted like those who starve,
nor desperate. For us were the orderly rows of corn, the tight cluster
of farm buildings. Our barns were clean and painted white, bright white.
No one was going to find a blemish, an opening, a crooked row,
a reason. For the most part, outsiders would not see us, and
when they did, they would see only perfection.

And now what has happened to you? Some of the ancestors
are not pleased. They fear for you; some fear for themselves.
They would tell you not to be messy and bold. Don't take us down
with you, they say. But listen to me. We oldest ones remember: The dying
was worth it, every pain. We were chosen to bring something new
into the world. They had to keep us from singing. They had to keep us
from singing.

Julia Kasdorf

Julia Kasdorf received national recognition as a poet from both outside and inside the Mennonite community when she won the Agnes Lynch Starrett Poetry Prize for *Sleeping Preacher*, her first full-length collection of poetry, in 1992. Kasdorf's *Sleeping Preacher* juxtaposes two worlds — as represented by New York and Big Valley, Pennsylvania — to create a third thing: a larger imaginative space that could contain both. While *Sleeping Preacher* deals with the body of the community and the circulation of its stories, *Eve's Striptease* (1998) chronicles the journey of a young girl as she matures through her sensual awakening to the world and her own desires. Kasdorf further explores the relationship between her poetic voice and Mennonite heritage in a collection of essays, *The Body and the Book: Writing from a Mennonite Life* (2001). Her biography of Joseph W. Yoder, a Big Valley writer who also tried to bridge the worlds of literature and Amish heritage, appeared in 2002.

Born Julia Spicher in 1962 in Lewistown, Pennsylvania, Julia moved with her family to suburban Pittsburgh when she was three years old. Her father was raised in an Old Order Amish family but joined the Conservative Conference Mennonite Church as a young man. In Pittsburgh, the family attended a Mennonite church frequented by students and professors at the university and later Scottdale Mennonite Church. Kasdorf spent two years at Goshen College. She then moved to New York City where she earned an M.A. in creative writing and a Ph.D. in English education from New York University. Here she also met and married David Kasdorf, a visual artist. They have one daughter. After teaching for several years at Messiah College, Kasdorf now directs the creative writing program at Pennsylvania State University. Her work has been widely anthologized and has appeared in many publications, including the *New Yorker*, *Pleiades*, *Poetry*, *Indiana Review*, and *Spoon River Quarterly*.

Mennonites

We keep our quilts in closets and do not dance.
We hoe thistles along fence rows for fear
we may not be perfect as our Heavenly Father.
We clean up his disasters. No one has to
call; we just show up in the wake of tornadoes
with hammers, after floods with buckets.
Like Jesus, the servant, we wash each other's feet
twice a year and eat the Lord's Supper,
afraid of sins hidden so deep in our organs
they could damn us unawares,
swallowing this bread, his body, this juice.
Growing up, we love the engravings in *Martyrs Mirror*:
men drowned like cats in burlap sacks,
the Catholic inquisitors,
the woman who handed a pear to her son,
her tongue screwed to the roof of her mouth
to keep her from singing hymns while she burned.
We love Catherine the Great and the rich tracts
she gave us in the Ukraine, bright green winter wheat,
the Cossacks who torched it, and Stalin,
who starved our cousins while wheat rotted
in granaries. We must love our enemies.
We must forgive as our sins are forgiven,
our great-uncle tells us, showing the chain
and ball in a cage whittled from one block of wood
while he was in prison for refusing to shoulder
a gun. He shows the clipping from 1916:
Mennonites are German milksops, too yellow to fight.
We love those Nazi soldiers who, like Moses,
led the last cattle cars rocking out of the Ukraine,
crammed with our parents — children then —
learning the names of Kansas, Saskatchewan, Paraguay.
This is why we cannot leave the beliefs
or what else would we be? why we eat
'til we're drunk on shoofly and moon pies and borscht.
We do not drink; we sing. Unaccompanied on Sundays,
those hymns in four parts, our voices lift with such force
that we lift, as chaff lifts toward God.

The Body Remembers

for David

Before they were married, Opa slept
on the floor beside Oma's bed.
The wedding feast was just
cabbage soup, not a bone
to cook in the village.
Even in Canada, Oma stewed borscht
without beef. In California, among orchards,
your mother cooks *geschmuade Bonen*
without ham. The body remembers
famine, but I make *Kartoffelsuppe*
thick with cream and stroke
your white ribs with my lips.
I kiss your stomach, innocent as a fish,
and crush my small, olive breasts
on your chest. The blades
of our pelvises collide
in defiance of grief
as we pull and thrust
against all the suffering
sown in our cells, all those stories
of bodies enduring torture and hunger
for God. We knock together
like two muddy shoes, knocking
history loose from our limbs,
knocking through Zurich and Danzig,
knocking off kulak and milksop
(all the names they once called us),
knocking until we are nothing special,
just a woman and a man on a floor
in Brooklyn, where Arab melodies
and Burmese cooking waft
through our windows like ghosts.

What I Learned from My Mother

I learned from my mother how to love
the living, to have plenty of vases on hand
in case you have to rush to the hospital
with peonies cut from the lawn, black ants
still stuck to the buds. I learned to save jars
large enough to hold fruit salad for a whole
grieving household, to cube home-canned pears
and peaches, to slice through maroon grape skins
and flick out the sexual seeds with a knife point.
I learned to attend viewings even if I didn't know
the deceased, to press the moist hands
of the living, to look in their eyes and offer
sympathy, as though I understood loss even then.
I learned that whatever we say means nothing,
what anyone will remember is that we came.
I learned to believe I had the power to ease
awful pains materially like an angel.
Like a doctor, I learned to create
from another's suffering my own usefulness, and once
you know how to do this, you can never refuse.
To every house you enter, you must offer
healing: a chocolate cake you baked yourself,
the blessing of your voice, your chaste touch.

Eve's Striptease

Lingerie shopping with Mom, I braced myself
for the wedding night advice. Would I seem
curious enough, sufficiently afraid? Yet
when we sat together on their bed, her words
were surprisingly wise:
                    Whatever happens, remember this —
                    it keeps getting better and better.
She had to be telling the truth. At ten,
I found a jar of Vaseline in her nightstand,

its creamy grease gouged deep, and dusting
their room each week, I marked the decline
of bedside candles. But she didn't say lust
is a bird of prey or tell me the passion
she passed on to me is no protector of borders.
She'd warned me only about the urges men get
and how to save myself from them. Though
she'd flirt with any greenhouse man
for the best cabbage flats, any grease monkey
under the hood, she never kissed anyone but Dad.
How could she guess that with *Jesus Loves Me*
on my tongue, constantly suffering crushes
on uncles, I would come to find that
almost everything gets better and better?
The tiny bird she set loving in me must
keep on, batting the bars of its cage
in a rage only matched by my cravings
for an ample pantry and golden anniversary.
She let me learn for myself all the desires
a body can hold, how they grow stronger
and wilder with age, tugging in every direction
until it feels like my sternum might split
like Adam's when Eve stepped out,
sloughing off ribs.

Poetry in America

The Barnes and Noble in Evansville, Indiana, mostly sells coffee
though the manager said ten or twelve showed up once for a local author.
One, besides my friend Laura, came for me. I thought of priests
who must pronounce the full Eucharist even if no one goes to mass,
thought Virginia Woolf and Oscar Wilde looked kind of pained
as Barnes and Noble posters, and facing fifteen empty folding chairs,
I suggested we all just go downstairs for coffee. I was hopeful —
I hate bookstore readings which pay nothing but constant interruptions:
Customer service on line eight. Does one keep reading in that case, or pause
to incorporate the line into her poem? "No way! I came to hear poetry!"
said a woman in walking shorts and sandals with socks. "I'm a poet, too.

Can't help the disease. It's either write or go mad." She had bangs
and plastic glasses like Ramona the Pest. "I'm Barbara. Don't write
much now, too busy working and labor organizing at the Whirlpool plant.
Come from Henderson, Kentucky, over the river. You hear of a white person
committing a crime in Henderson, that would be my relative.
But let's get going. I've got things to do yet tonight." So I got going.

Sometimes Barbara moaned as if she'd tasted something delicious or cried,
"Hey, that was a good one." People walking by eyed us the way
they look at preachers in bus stations. A woman and little girl sat in back.
The Mom held a book about women who love too much in front of her face
like a mask, the girl imitated with a Madeline storybook, but sometimes
she peeked at me, and they stayed almost to the end. Barbara took my book
from the stack waiting to be returned. "Wouldn't buy it if I didn't like the
    work,"
she said as I signed, then walked out with us. "You know, it's still 73 cents
to the dollar. No matter how much education you have, you're working
    harder
and making less than a white man. For women of color, it's worse.
And now all we get is backlash. Well, I'm a 50-year-old woman, and
they can kiss my ass." That spring, Barbara fasted for 19 days at the gates
of the governor's mansion because he'd turned Kentucky's community
    colleges
into trade schools. "Do you know what that means?" she jabbed me with
    her bird eyes.
"No history, no political science, no literature, no going on for a college
    degree
like I did, and you watch, it's coming to other states. Evil bastards will call it
job training, but it's just one more way to keep poor people down." Outside,
light mist was falling on cars in the parking lot, softening neon signs down
    the strip.
"Take care of yourself," she waved a blessing. "Where the hell is your
    umbrella?"

Audrey Poetker

Audrey Poetker was born in 1962 in Steinbach, Manitoba, and is descended from both Kanadier and Russlander grandparents, terms designating Mennonite immigrants to Canada from Russia in the 1870s and 1920s, respectively. She attended a Mennonite church in rural Manitoba with her parents until she was fifteen, but now considers herself to be only culturally Mennonite. Poetker has lived in rural Manitoba for most of her life, except for a year in the former East Germany and several months in France. She is married to Jack Thiessen, a retired professor of German known for his humorous Mennonite short stories in Low German.

Poetker's poems have been published in a variety of journals, including *Prairie Fire, New Quarterly, Canadian Literature*, and *Border Crossings*. She is the author of three collections of poetry: *i sing for my dead in german* (1986), *standing all the night through* (1992), and *Making Strange to Yourself* (1999), all published by Turnstone Press. *standing all the night through* was nominated for the McNally Robinson Manitoba Book of the Year Award in 1992.

Poetker's poetry is marked by a sparseness that intensifies language. Her poems concern, grief, loss, relationships, and the complexities of living in a Mennonite community. Countering traditional Mennonite logocentrism, she brings the physicality of human existence to the forefront in her poetry. Currently Poetker lives on a farm in rural Manitoba, where she is working on a novel.

she tries to tell him
this is one thing
hold on to it   like when
she was a girl she never
missed a dance   she picked
black-eyed susans   & tiger
lilies were wild as then

dancing & life   when did it
all become wrong
when she gave in to him
& put on her shoes when she hung
out the wash   or when
he became a deacon   making her
a wife with a dryer
& a deacon

who needs a dryer when
her strong thin line binds
trees together   keeps the leaves
from unravelling   the sound
wind makes against her apron
gathered for clothespins
the sound of her hair rushing
free from its bun
this fine wind   clear heat
& sunshine trapped forever
in the sheets between two
chokecherry trees

Symbols of Fertility

. . . things that are never satisfied
. . . the grave; and the barren womb . . .
— *Proverbs*

1.

My lover wears only boxer shorts.
He is not allowed to ride bikes
or horses; he avoids saunas and hot tubs.
He is always ready when my temperature is.

I have touched the Robe of Christ
at the cathedral in Trier.
I have imbibed wine in the gardens
in the Mosel Valley.
I have stood on my head
after sex, balanced delicately
against the wall.
I have burning, shining faith
up against the wall.

2.

My breasts, like my mother's good china,
have never been used. My mother's
good china is kept wrapped
in tissue paper, stored,
hedged against possibilities.
Perhaps someone important
will come to dinner.

Why, hello! Your Majesty!

Mirage. Fata Morgana.
My breasts describe
the shape of my sorrow.

3.

There is no shortage
of children in this world.

There is only a shortage
of children with my smile.

4.

What am I being punished for?
For years I have dreamt 3 dreams:
a dream of a narrow flight of stairs,
of a car driving backwards,
of a house burning down.
I am tormented, exhausted.
None of these dreams end well.
I am shivering with exhaustion.

5.

As the lion dreams Africa
and the dog dreams the rabbit
I dream the children

As the garden dreams the gardener
and the winter dreams the story
I dream the children

As the story dreams the truth
and the truth dreams the silence
I dream the children

As the silence dreams the lovers
and the children dream the breast
I dream the children

Fallen Women

The skeletons in this town are mostly
the bones of fallen women, the stories
you heard from your mother who heard
them from hers, or a little bird

Where there is grass there are
dandelions, where there are skeletons
there are women, fallen from grace
or from favour, bussing the empty
buffalo's head, the plowed prairie

You cannot resist the frivolous grace
of the bones. They rasp in the shadows
against the memory of flesh, sleep
sleep without sorrow.

My kingdom is of this world

the thin peeling of an orange, impertinent
earrings, the lightness of lilacs, the Carter
Family singing in the kitchen, my kingdom
is of this world, the dream that follows
and gladdens the day, I am glad for you

for Bev, for Ruth, for Dale, I am in
this world, I am of it, out of the familiar
rivers the body emerges copper, the earth
flirts with danger in its slow revolutions
in the scuttering darkness, there are

dusty roads that lead nowhere, thank god
for that, I have allowed myself beginnings
I have been foolish for love, curious
filled with questions, I have worn one
white glove for no reason at all, I have risen

at night, in my rapture, to admire the corn
the squash, the beans, I have been amazed
by the thunder, sunshine on mesas, surprised
by the flutes of Santa Fe, I have tasted blood
and skin and white sheets stained with love

the hairs on my neck have risen, I have been
shocked into song by men who love their wives
by the grace of it, the goodness, that some roads
lead somewhere, thank god, the world is my kingdom
I am in it, I am of it, you in me, I in you

love

Todd Davis

Born in Elkhart County, Indiana, in 1965 and raised there and in Ashfield, Massachusetts, Todd Davis has lived among and worshipped with Mennonites for most of his life, although he was not brought up as a Mennonite. Davis's poetry has been shaped by his father's profession as a veterinarian as well as by his mother's vocation as a lay minister in the United Methodist Church. While working with his father taught him about science, mortality, and hard work, accompanying his mother to churches where she preached developed Davis's respect for spirituality.

Davis received a B.A. from Grace College, where he won the English Department Award and played on the basketball team. He received his M.A. and Ph.D. in English from Northern Illinois University, where he studied with the Zen Buddhist poet Lucien Stryk. Davis taught English and creative writing at Goshen College from 1996 to 2002. He served as a writer in residence in the creative writing program at Iowa State University in 2002–2003. At present he teaches creative writing, American literature, and environmental studies at Penn State Altoona. Davis is the author of *Ripe*, a collection of poetry (2002). His poems have appeared in *Appalachia, Blueline, The Mid-America Poetry Review, Black Dirt, Farmer's Market, Red Cedar Review*, and *Image: A Journal of Art and Religion*. Married and the father of two sons, Davis is a member of the College Mennonite Church in Goshen, Indiana.

Ripe

North Manitou Island, Lake Michigan

The northern woods are fat,
as are the deer who walk
the beaches at dusk and dawn.

Sugar maples, striped maples,
beech and birch put out
leaves large as hands.

Blackberry vines droop,
heavy with berries dark
as the sky to the north

where the lights of towns
to the south do not reach.
In late August, there is nothing

that cannot be gleaned:
mushrooms, apples, nuts,
the ripeness that precedes

the day when the very earth
turns away from the sun,
when ice forms at the edge

of the shore and deer stop
bedding in open meadows,
abandoned orchards,

when they head toward
the center of the island,
find hemlock groves, gather

together as best they can.
Come spring those
who survive will rise

from melting snow, as will
the fawn mushrooms whose soft
haunches lift around the rotting

bodies of deer whose hunger
could not wait for the return
of warm, green rains.

Elkhart, Indiana

When I was seventeen,
in the factory town where I lived,
each Friday the sons of the dispossessed —
Hungarians, Italians, Mexicans,
Poles and Greeks, and Blacks whose fathers
had come north to work the line —
ventured out under field lights
to run violently toward
the only thing that made sense.

Marked by chalk and posts,
the end zone offered a safety
we could find no place else,
and there we danced with anger:
the terrible beauty of our bodies
blossoming as we threw ourselves
head-first toward the dark
that lay just beyond this circle of light.

That was the last fine time, before love
and violence grew tired, spent and bare
like the scratched turf at the center of the field.
On those nights, while our families shouted
from the stands, their cries indistinguishable
from the darkness, we wondered for the briefest
of moments about the year after next.

Building Walls

At the edge of our woods,
when the trees begin to green
and you say
> it is time to go for stone,
> the rocks begin to surface.

They grow large in surrounding fields,
backs of the baptized
cleaned by storms,
> and their weight, pushing toward blue,
> settles darkly.

In late afternoon we sweat
with the effort of moving stone from earth
while spring sun,
> still pushed to the far horizon,
> begins to take our working light.

Rusted wheelbarrow carries what will be today's last load,
and together, where our field ends and the world begins,
we touch,
> shoulder to shoulder,
> fitting stone upon stone.

Letter to My Mother, Sixteen Years after the Fact

I thought it was high time
to tell you what I did
at summer camp.

Don't worry,
it doesn't involve girls
in bathing suits at the beach,
long fingers pulling elastic
down around the soft flesh
of their bottoms, contrast
of white on brown.

Or the unsure dreams of sex
that I woke from with regret
and longing, embarrassed
by the tautness of my skin,
the throbbing that sent me
to the bathroom stalls.

It doesn't concern boys
driving fast in cars
whose engines ached for speed.
Flat road stretching on
through cornfields into the night,
toward the faint glow
of some other Indiana town
where we could buy cheap beer,
pretend that the suds
absolved us of our youth,
make like men back to Warsaw:
Head lamps spreading light,
fog slipping from riverbeds
in search of misfortune.

What I did was walk through the dark
to Center Lake where the concrete pier
cuts through water, clapping of waves
sounding against its sides, and there I climbed
the ladder to the diving board that hung
fifteen feet above the black body
of night, curtain of water covering
this hollow place in the earth.
I looked down, remembering your stories
of teenagers who dove into unknown waters,
their lives ended tragically or spent in wheelchairs.
Then I pitched myself head first, arms splayed
as I'd been taught at the YMCA,
pushed my fingers forward at dive's end,
waited for water to swallow me.

Loving the Flesh

How surprised we are to find we live here,
Here within our bodies.
—Eric Pankey

Last night I lay beside you, unable to sleep,
and read the stories written on my cells by one
who long ago breathed into dust, shaped flesh
from earth and deemed it good, who set me
in the boat of my mother's womb rocking.
How could I imagine a heaven without
these legs, these arms, this heart that beats
inside the cage of my chest, blood pumping
outward like the first days when sap rises
to meet the warmth of some late winter sun?

Tonight after dinner as we spoke to one another
in that careless, sleepy way we do when the children
have left us with nothing more than our love
and its weariness, you told me that the things
of this world were far too heavy for you to carry
into the next, that you hoped one day death
would be a move toward something better, like leaving
an old house with no more than a backward glance.

But what of the pear, I said, whose perfect skin shines
in the basket by the window, and what of Christ
who could not leave this earth without his love
for the woman who drew water from the well,
without first cooking fish for those he knew
could never hold fast — cool breeze of morning
coming onto shore, bread warming hands
that still ached from holes not yet healed, fire burnt
down to a circle of coal and ash.

Now going up the stairs to our room I think
about how tomorrow morning the rabbit will leave
his den, how the early light will move against the far wall
and we will wake to each other's body, how you will allow
me to kiss the top of your head, line of scar near the corner

of your mouth, the narrow bone of your shoulder blade
that peeks out from under your gown, your breasts
that tip away from your chest, like our minds when we forget
that we would not know a soul if it were not draped by skin
and muscle, by tendon upon bone, by artery and vein entwined.

David Wright

David Wright was born in 1966 in Urbana, Illinois, and grew up near Peoria, Illinois, where he attended a variety of mainline and evangelical churches. As a high school student, he became involved with a Mennonite youth group, where he renewed his wavering Christian commitments. He graduated with a B.A. in English from Millikin University and received his M.A. in English from Northeast Missouri State University. He is completing a Ph.D. at Loyola University; his dissertation explores the poetics of community in the work of Wendell Berry, Gwendolyn Brooks, Denise Levertov, Carolyn Forché, and Jeff Gundy. His study of community and his pacifist convictions led him toward the Anabaptist tradition, and he joined the First Mennonite Church in Urbana, Illinois, in 1997. He currently attends the Lombard Mennonite Church in Lombard, Illinois. Wright lives in the Chicago area with his wife and daughter and teaches English at Wheaton College.

Wright has published scholarship and reviews in the *Midwest Quarterly*, *re:generation quarterly*, and the *Mennonite Quarterly Review*. His poetry has appeared in the *Mars Hill Review*, *Green Hills Literary Lantern*, *Christian Century*, *Rolling Coulter*, the *Mennonite*, and other magazines. His poem "A New Mennonite Replies to Julia Kasdorf" juxtaposes traditional ethnic Mennonite language and experiences with more contemporary manifestations of Mennonite identity. A new collection of poetry, *A Liturgy for Stones*, appeared in 2003.

A New Mennonite Replies to Julia Kasdorf

This is why we cannot leave the beliefs
or what else could we be?
—*Julia Kasdorf, from "Mennonites"*

As best I can tell, most of our quilts here were inherited,
or bought at relief sales, spread on guest beds,
displayed on polished oak racks. Not much borscht,
few shoofly pies at potlucks — instead it's
hummus, free range chicken, carob brownies.
No bacon-laced bean casserole. Someone
steamed soy beans last Sunday, right in the pods.

Maundy Thursday we wash each other's hands.
It is optional, so I stay seated,
beside a Lutheran woman, Harvard
theologian, and we wish together
for liturgy because we cannot play
the name game. Neither can my agnostic
Quaker friend. We drink coffee on Mondays
to talk politics instead. Between fields,
one of our farmers, ex-Amish Otto
brother, teaches medieval Catholic
thinkers whose names I can never recall.

So many new and remade and restless
and not-quite Mennonites, driving Volvos
and minivans. We park ourselves in pews
next to women and men who know better
what real Mennonites really are, at least
have usually been, who tolerate us
when we do not know (or want to) the so
many stories we should. Some seem amused,
some even grieved, others simply angry
that our martyr stories come in children's
sermons where Dirk rescues and is killed right
next to Rosa Parks and Ruby Bridges,
where Luther himself nails necessary
correctives on Wittenberg's door.

We sing,
though, a solid four parts; the hymns here have
a sturdy bottom (though I need the book
on 606). And we make our way through
less solid but sweet guitar-sent songs
your great uncles would never recognize.
Our preacher never swoons. He's biblical,
careful, and knows the university
crowd listens each week. Once, he prayed, "May God
bless your mind's wanderings." Which go now to
China Buffet, where two tables away
a woman wears heavy head covering
and pale green dress as she eats with her son.
I say to Becky, "Should we tell her?" "What?"
"That we're Mennonites too?" Becky smiles, licks
sugar from her fingers, the residue
of deep fried dough passing here for ethnic
dessert. "Maybe we could tell her we're new
at it?" God bless our wandering, indeed.

Addison Street

A small, rounded woman sits next to me. She is gumming sunflower seeds.
    Her lips close and click like the clasps on a purse. She makes a
    comic face, like my infant daughter tasting peaches for the first
    time. We stop, just past Wrigley Field, old, green, and empty.

She reaches into her enormous, crinkled plastic seed bag. She fills her hand,
    then fills her mouth, the entire handful at once. She cannot
    contain them all in the gathers and folds of her pleated cheeks.
    She coughs. Seeds scatter from her lips. A shower of shells
    splatters my arm.

No seeds take root. Not one of them bursts into a small sun, or anything
    beautiful at all.

She reaches her slim fingers towards me, without hesitation and picks a
    seed from my skin.

She licks off the salt and flicks the seed back into her mouth.
  She does not look at my face, but I look at hers, see her cheeks
  churn like a squirrel's.

She gleans another full seed from my arm, fixes it on her lips, squeezes
  them together and forces the oily heart onto her tongue. We
  hurtle, at last, to her stop.

She stands to leave, and sputters a coarse laugh, like static, before she spits.

She has swallowed the salty husks and strewn the gray, lifeless seeds at my feet.

A Map of the Kingdom

You are not far from the kingdom of God.
—*Mark 12:34*

How near to the borders can we venture,
How close to the looming or invisible walls
  Without being taken, trapped like wild game,
  Netted like unsuspecting fish that hover in their own blue kingdom
  To be suddenly tangled then yanked high into a world of light and air?

Some creatures love to be sought, not found,
  Love to be caught, not bound,
  To be lured within range,
  Never quite aware of where the net
  Has cast itself — much wider than we suspect.

Perhaps our sore lips already speak the language of this nearby land.
  Listen. It almost sounds like plainchant.
  Or jazz. An anthem, a cadence
  To coax and measure our steps.

  We should watch where we walk.
  We should watch what we say.

  A kingdom of margins will find us.
  God's grammar is not far from our tongues.

Beethoven's Romance in G

Here is why we listen:
    a fifteen year old boy
    who will not yet have mangled
    his heart in the barbed wire
    of loss and desire
    can sing violin strings
    through humid air
    so the deaf man's
    beautiful wound heals aloud,
    above and within us.
    Hands on a fretless neck
    and bow on stretched string
    vibrate his narrow shoulders,
    echo under his slim, clean
    fingers. The sound moves,
    presses grooves, cuts and grows
    through his still body and eyes,
    where he can only imagine
    the fresh and worn scars of love.
    But he can hear and bless
    the air with lucid sound
    that filters through fences
    unassaulted and free,
    and, in this morning,
    saves and releases
    what will be graceful
    tomorrow and in memory,
    even after being sifted
    through the sieves of ourselves.

A Protest Poem

after watching Jesse Jackson march in Decatur

I fit storm windows, hammer odd
corners to force them into frames
that have settled, not square. The news
heralds this old ambassador,
missionary, activist who
can argue justice, stand between
intransigent minds — generals
and rebels with blood on their boots.
His marchers sing, carrying signs
righteous enough to make headlines,
become news for a day, sound byte
of a pure, just cause. Balanced on
one foot, arms stretching past their reach,
I hang the metal eyes over
their hooks, small and tight connections,
strong enough to last the winter.
The whole house holds itself in place
by these thousand, thousand little
joints, nails, beads of caulk and mortar
wearing to decay, each at its
own speed. Marching, chanting, old, new
warriors link arms for the camera's
short and jaded gaze. It watches
for moments when cities, countries
come apart. Behind the glass, I
wait, write, mind the television
with one eye, look out the window
with the other. What space divides.
I see the street from the house. They
know the house from the road. But some
of both will be here, putting on screens
again next spring, making gardens
along the boulevard if we
can pull together seed and tools
enough to tend shoots like children.
They may not even know they want,
or need, to bloom here, take root deep

where tornadoes drop from clouds,
where history erupts beneath
the homes and streets, tearing rooted
and rootless away from the earth.
Glass rattles through the benign night.
Darkness rests on particular
homes, settled and coming apart,
unless the owners can take care.

Barbara Nickel

Born in Saskatoon, Saskatchewan, in 1966, Barbara Kathleen Nickel was raised in a Mennonite community in Rosthern, Saskatchewan. She graduated from Goshen College, where she studied violin with Lon Sherer, to whom her first book of poetry, *The Gladys Elegies*, is dedicated. Nickel received an M.F.A. in creative writing from the University of British Columbia and edited the journal *PRISM International* while she was a student there.

Nickel has won awards for her poems, including the *Malahat Review*'s Long Poem Contest and the Pat Lowther Memorial Award. She is also an accomplished writer of fiction and authored an award-winning book for young readers, *The Secret Wish of Nannerl Mozart*. She currently teaches violin and writes in British Columbia.

Lines

I. ESCAPE

The empty foolscap,
the instructions; write
I will not lie to Mrs. Hanson
100 times while they skate.

I can't, so I
fumble with boot laces,
my skin meets the air
at forty below zero, running
home for my skates, my head's
bowing down I want

I want to stop. Stop, make
an angel in the snow,
deep wings wide and clean —

II. IN CHURCH

Russia, 1918.
Great grandfather Johann J. behind
the Chortitza Mennonite pulpit preaching;
Wenn Christus seine Kirche schutzt,
So mach die Hölle wuten —

his words turn to steam, to
beads hanging from
Gerhard Thiessen's beard.
He's not listening, who is, nobody, all
hunched and stiff on hard pews thinking
about the gun pointed at
Jacob Friesen's head, 400 rubles
and all the food stolen:
butter, eggs, flour, ham.

Thinking about bandits
burning down the Bergmann estate
and raping the daughters, thinking
about tonight, which Mennonite family

will hear the pounding hooves, lick
of fire, curse of smashed glass?
Whose farm the anarchists' promised land?

—*Er der zu rechten Gottes sitzt,*
Hat Macht ihr zu erbieten.

Great grandfather closes his Bible.

Relief of standing, escape
in a four-part hymn, terror
forgotten in the pooling
voices, the one huge sound.

Father, I'm joining the White Army —
says Isaak, my grandfather, on the way home.

The wind sucks his words into a snow drift.

Johann J. nods, thinking
about the congregation, how
today they looked like cattle
ready for slaughter.

III. LAMENT FOR MARGARETHA

Isaak, nine, at his mother's coffin.
He wants to hide his face in her bosom again,
smell her bread rising, he wants
her strong fingers stroking his hair, wants her
in the house where she belongs,
at table, her voice
kneading them together,
their hands joined, singing the grace.

Isaak bows his head, stares at her white face.

His father marries Maria. All spindly
limbs she marches into the kitchen, she's
always cleaning, shooing
her broom at Isaak with
his dirty boots, with his runny nose.
Away with you Isaak,

go on with you,
outside with you, go
make yourself clean.

IV. ESCAPE

I want to make an angel
but I run home. Need
my skates, need to
get to the rink. Cold sun
in my eyes, snow drifts, white
road. The insides
of my thighs rub against
each other but there's only
a tiny hurt with each step, bits
of fingers and toes,
tips of ears.

V. ESCAPE

Russia, 1919.
Isaak in the White Army stabs
at heroics, misses, gets
typhus. On the old wagon, he sees white sky.
Uncle Jake covers him with
a fur coat, the left boot exposed.

Then the shame, left toes full of
frostbite and gangrene, amputation.
He tries to limp home, sleeps on
frozen cowshit in some abandoned
barn, is captured by the Red Army.
Their gun to his head, he says
he's one of them, escapes, limps to
Chortitza in the numbing
of hands, nose,
his five good toes.

For shame, Maria would say.

Isaak thaws among his sisters Katharina, Elizabeth,
Anna, Emily. Father Johann prays.
His eyes shut Isaak out
bow him down.

VI. ESCAPE

I can't turn the door handle
so punch the bell, door opening,
Mom. *I need my skates.* She rubs
my hands warm. Dad's behind the table
sipping coffee, high up
as that icicle in the eaves, its
tip I can't reach.

VII. ON THE FARM

Saskatchewan, 1941.
Isaak my grandfather views his fields,
the stubble poking through that
dirty white sea, wind freezing
his ears, nose, five toes.
The barn creaks and dogs bark.
What will you do? Drought, *what?*
Crop damage, low prices and
the dogs fight over a white, dry bone.
What will you do?
He storms inside with the wind.

Arnold my dad plays horse with
the Sunday shoes, tying the laces together.

Time for chores.

The wind carries my grandfather's voice.

Listen to me, I said time for chores, hear?

Grandfather grabs my dad's ear,
jerks him to his feet, twists it hot.

My dad fumbles with his boot laces
in the dark hallway.

VIII. ESCAPE

Dad drives me to the rink.
I clutch my skates, a hot
blast on my cheeks and Mozart
on the CBC mock me, say *everything's OK.*
The rink door creaking and a smell
of dark wood and cigarettes,
greasy fries. I watch
my friends skate while
Dad talks to Mrs. Hanson.
—100 lines —
— lied to me —
— ran home —
— lied, lied, lied —

By the station wagon, Dad pulls
down my pants, the hard
of his hand hits
me over and over, my snot
waters the dog pee
on the snow below.

I love you,
says my dad, helping me
blow my nose, wipe my eyes.

IX. POLKA

I love you too.

But I do,

the hospital smell
of him when he comes home and I curl up
under the afghan beside him, the feel of his wood
carvings and the way he listens
to my music, swerves the car around crazy
and wears yellow long underwear, posing as a banana.

I love to polka with him at dances, the hard floor
and all the people with it slipping out
from under us, only Dad and me and the wild

Ukrainian music left, turning around and around, wet
and breathless and dizzy, our feet
stamping to the wild music, stamping
the generations down and down.

Three Poems for Violin

PRACTICE

At five each day I watch sun ignite
air-dust in this corner to a swarm
of gnats the metronome's steel finger swats,
while giant flowered armchairs stalk the room.
My violin is a skinny girl.
I tap the measured belly, ribs, neck;
strings pulley me, cross-eyed, beyond the scroll.
Father shrugs his paper. Mother cooks.
My scales pinch the winter afternoon and slide
off-key, whine like children lost at fairs.
Mistake. I want to break cracker-thin wood
and see it burn, limbs turning blue in fire.
Instead I watch the dust gnats glint
and pick the hardened sore beneath my chin.

COMPETITION

I'm next. Fright spurts through me, threading
a way pricked by stares. The bow scuttles
across the strings. Music is a bead
inside my chest — it rises to my skull,
says, *Let me out.* I only feel a shaking,
new breasts that hurt like pinpoints underneath
the ruffle that my mother sewed. Bouquets
inflame the doors on every side. I breathe
and wait for judgement final as a knot.
You lost, the pencils blurt. I want a voice
unravelling, a spiral from my throat,
a curve unfurling, loose as silken floss.

Outside, the broken step, the smell of thaw;
a crocus like a bruise in muddy snow.

BUSKING

We play near aging cheese and scattered rice,
among the pumpkins, gulls and smell of fish,
breezes, clatter jesting on my face,
the jostles of the crowd and passing swish
of silk unseen. Our lines of music join
the cappuccino screams, juggle above
a pile of ripe tomatoes; seeds spill down,
and juice and music mash up in a sieve;
Mozart, the people shout. I laugh as doors
open, wind snatching notes and rumpling clothes.
Our cases on the wet and sticky floor,
the clinking coins on velvet, crumpled bills.
Beside my violin, a tiny boy
is moving to the shadow of my joy.

Carmen Horst

Carmen Susana Horst was born in 1971 in the Argentine Chaco to Mennonite missionaries. She spent most of her formative years in Argentina until she entered Goshen College. Her names reveal the combination of Argentine and Mennonite cultural influences on her identity. A bilingual awareness of language has been a formative part of Horst's vision as a poet as well as in her work as a medical interpreter.

While at Goshen College, Horst studied poetry writing with Nick Lindsay and published a book of poetry in Spanish and English with Pinchpenny Press, *like the cicada/como la cigarra*, in 1994. In the same year she also edited an anthology of broadsides published at Goshen, *A Whistle over the Water*, with Wanda Kraybill. Horst has recently studied poetry in writing workshops with Ron Wallace and Jesse Lee Kercheval at the University of Wisconsin-Madison. She is working toward an M.A. in Christian spirituality at Associated Mennonite Biblical Seminaries. She received the George B. Hill 2000 Poetry Prize from the program in creative writing at the University of Wisconsin-Madison for "Ugly Poem" and "Siesta."

Interpreter

It is important work.
But it has nothing to do with mission.
Nothing to do with bridges.
It is more like preparing the egg
for Pysanky, that painstaking Ukrainian art.
She sits, painted for the occasion. People
lean in with all their intentions.

She is sick of their lips on her
lips hates their fat plushy
lips that open and close and blow, out
slips her quick rosy heart, her brain
like a coiled and silvery cabbage she
is tired of their hands on her hands
lips on her lips lips on her ears long
after she's empty.

Afterwards,
she walks aimless, a doll,
limbs strung together by brown rubber bands
taut in the shadows of her echoing torso:
arm to hard molded plastic arm,
leg to leg in their shifty sockets.
She wants to lie down,
let all the limbs loll.
They detatch as she walks, jerk at the joints,
she snaps them back like lagging attention.

She sleeps as if she will never wake,
dreams blue luminous bulging veins,
old black and white reel tapes of fluids.
Valves gushing gringo verbiage. A click,
and the rush of Spanish sewage.
She dreams black eyes swimming in blue eyes,
lips floating in the Panama Canal,
locks mechanically filling and falling,
as the helpless shapes of the oceans change.

Siesta

In the cool dark behind the blinds,
behind the shutters, every eye sleeps.
The avocado tree drops her hands

and a tear-shaped fruit, and waits.
Dishes stand in clean uniform rows
like school children. A bell keeps

the hour. Only the white refrigerator goes,
humming quietly about its work
like an old British missionary everybody knows

and takes for granted. Teenagers neck
on dappled benches downtown,
or buzz their motorbikes up the ten blocks

of the empty main avenue and around
the plaza. The river, with a sigh
sweeps the curb of the drowsy town,

pushing swill from east Paraguay,
afternoon moon and water hyacinth,
shuffles and waves good-bye, good-bye.

Ugly Poem

I will not write about our bodies in the gray dawn, calm and awake as
   trees. I will not mention the tremendous thing that happened in the
   sky as the sun was rising.

I will write about the nice middle class neighborhood all up in arms
   because fifteen Mexicans have moved into the Morgan house. A house
   needs one bedroom

for every two people, so that the neighbors can sleep comfortably. I
   will tell about the new Wal-Mart going up across from the old one
   that's too small, about

the *yanqui* sweatshops in Tijuana where you get three dollars a day and
fired for being pregnant. I will tell you about crawling for three nights
across the hills

between searchlights, hearing someone fall over the edge in the dark and
thanking God it wasn't you. I will talk about tires slashed as if they
were sugar cane, forests

slashed as if they were sugar cane, jobs slashed because they are sugar
cane. Since this is an ugly poem, I will not tell you about César
whispering in my ear in

the hall, "*Maestra*, thank you for saying something to me in Spanish,"
or the steaming *moles* from his mother that show up on my desk and
doorstep. Instead, I

will tell you what I think when he turns: *Be very careful, César, I may be
your worst enemy.* I take your hand and show you kindly to the room of
forgetfulness, where

you will hate Spanish, the memory of your *abuelita's* farm, and your very
own name. In this poem I will not say that the tongue is a deep muscle
connected

directly to the emotions. I will say nothing of the blossoms on my African
violet, their deep purple like the sound of bells. Instead I will tell of
fluent tongues

extracted gently, like slivers, from the trembling mouth, of days of rage,
when like my mother, I can't stop crying or chopping onions, when
living is facing a great

white wall, tongue parched, ears ringing, the glare in your open eyes.

Everything I Know

Everything I know about you, Grandma Susie,
whose name is tucked into my own Susana,
I learned on visits to Ohio I can count on one hand.
We stopped at the last gas station in Youngstown,
shucked off old jeans in the flourescent restroom,
emerged braided, skirted, and ready to meet our makers.
While Grandpa napped, you sat with Dad
watching birds squabble at the winter feeder.
I rolled marbles and listened to long silences.
I studied your hand-painted birthday calendar
for the names of the newest cousins,
checked for our same list of six, shrinking
among all those fertile families of fourteen.

The rest of what I know Dad has told me.
How you welcomed him home from his Florida road trip,
embraced that flaming red shirt he'd bought
twinkling, "That's a pretty bright shirt, now, Willis."
How Dad cleaned the family bumpers once
to show the shiny chrome, and Grandpa,
without a word, painted those bumpers black again.
And Dad cleaned them, and Grandpa painted them.
Before long, Dad would leave for college,
and his bishop brother, the uncle I've never seen,
would dismiss him from the Lord's Table and his own.

But there's another story, before all that.
You climb the back stairs to the boys' bedroom,
arms loaded with dark, clean shirts and socks.
My father cradles his worldly guitar
in that brief window between school and chores.
You smile and whisper like a blessing,
"David and his harp," as you pass by.

Swimming

for Mary L.

A red dragonfly darts, little
sharp tongue. The bluegill
keeps an eye on me all through July
circles the sandy bowl of his nest.
The kingfisher wears a stole on her breast.
For years I've been searching:
Which word in which of my languages
spoken over this body would bring it back?
Above me, the pumping arrow
of a heron, wind idling in the cottonwoods,
bank swallows whirling into a dive.
Nothing below but dark, dangerous water,
its familiar resistance, yield and caress.
Later, I think of baptism, birth —
all the obvious parallels.
Later I understand my body's blessing,
the translation she has been murmuring for me:
Remember? That old embrace of water,
the swallows flinging themselves on the afternoon
air, mean something like, *Do not fear.*

Jessica Smucker Falcón

Jessica Smucker was born in Lancaster County, Pennsylvania, in 1977 into a Mennonite family, grew up in the village of Bird-in-Hand, and attended Lancaster Mennonite High School. She has been a writer from a very young age and began to write poetry seriously during her teens. After several years at Goshen College and a variety of jobs — including gardener, bookstore employee, journalist, and web designer — Smucker received a B.A. in English and creative writing from Western Illinois University, where she studied with Tama Baldwin. While a student, Smucker self-published a chapbook, *How the Light Gets In*. Her work has appeared in the *Spoon River Poetry Review*, *Aura Literary Arts Review*, the *Dirty Goat*, the *Mennonite*, and *turnrow*.

Smucker has found inspiration for her poetry from the discovery of her Navajo-Arapaho-Cheyenne roots when she was in college. Her marriage to Bryan Falcón, of Puerto Rican ancestry, promises an even more complex heritage for her descendants.

Hemispheres

If your right brain causes you to sin,
lobotomize.
Seat your men and boys on the left side of the sanctuary,
women on the right with their daughters
and suckling baby boys.

The congregation shall raise its voice
harmoniously
but in parallel lines
which, according to custom, never cross.

Your father lifts his ax
to chop you from your mother, severs the cord
like lightning strikes the telephone wire.

There are reasons why
you can't remember being born
apart from the physical trauma
of exodus
from mother's womb, through her widening channel,
into life.
In this promised land,
there are things you would still miss: uterine rays
emitting guileless warmth, a fist-like circle
closed around your nakedness, her garden of
coalescent cells, ripe curves
and the closeness of her breathy voice, contracting
with instruction.

Limp hemispheres
dangle from your center
like rope sausage —
the diversity of rib, tongue, buttocks
all blended into one
unchanging meat.

Are you not hungry?
Will you not eat?

Speak the language you never learned
to swallow. It's a bitter fruit
that's fallen from your mother's
Epicurean tree

but you have tasted so much sweetness
your stomach, teeth, breath and lips
are sour.

Won't you come back to the girding of the womb?
Slay the cherubim and seraphim who stand between
your right and left, your north and south,
your east and west —
the dragons you've hired as hit men
to harm you in your sin.

Won't you shed those garments of fig?

Listen to the wordless touch
of embryonic fluid, the rustle of the wind,
God walking through the garden.
You've toiled many years away, harvested the notion
that every leaf must one day detach
and fall —

Have you not heard of evergreens?
They stand tall, leaves intact, speak one language
every season, year after year.

Indian Locks

i

Mama had hips the shape of Iowa
a uterus as spacious as Wyoming

fetuses grew so comfortable
inside her
they dammed the birth canal
tied themselves to the uterine walls
to keep from being born

ii

I come from a long illegitimate line
of opossums playing dead
in the middle of the road

who did not know the center line
is to be traveled, not feared —
a line of blood

iii

Indians were myths in 1955
like unicorns
for Halloween, we dressed in buckskin moccasins
and feathers
and felt strangely like ourselves

iv

I dreamed you were a prophetess
among the Navajo
you spoke a language truer than tongues

v

Languages you never spoke,
languages with recessive genes:
    Arapaho
    Cheyenne

You learned English.

vi

History dries
its weight
pressed against
our silent tongues

buildings rise in the east
nature crumbles in the west

vii

Mama take this brush to your hair
comb out the men
who break and enter
through your Indian locks

they disgrace your leather moccasins
they do not know your name.

Sycamore

Sycamore stood in the middle of our backyard —
arms stretched to heaven, feet planted on the ground
resplendent and trapped
like Jesus

between everything and God.

Before we were tall enough to climb her branches,
my brother and I pared away her brittle bark.
Meekness in our fingers, we learned to compare

bark with skin.

We ripped her bark like hangnails and scabs,
tattooed her body with childish art —
secret hieroglyphics, the signature
of Jesus in the sand.

One day, Dad hung us by skinny arms
from the highest branch he could reach.
"To build your strength," he said and walked

impassively away, leaving us like Hansel and Gretl
at the mercy of a tree.
We wriggled like wet worms on a fisherman's hook
until cramps in our stomachs and salt in our eyes
became too much to bear.
Dad jumped up, then, from his watchman's post,
to save us, as we knew he would.
Limp as leaves, we fell into his arms.

The problem with roots, I now understand,
is this: by nature, *they stay.*
They are planted in the ground.
When you leave, fathers and trees,
unable to follow, wait
in the backyard for your return.

Does her loose bark still itch for me?
Does he trim her branches back every spring?
If I try to run home, will I still know the way?
If I shout the name of Jesus, will my soul be saved?

Now, I would surrender to her broken limbs.
I could fall and feel no pain.

Burial Clothes

I.

Grussy's body lay for three days
in the living room, dressed as she had dressed
alive: apron, shawl, black stockings.
Her covering strings relaxed about her breast.

We tiptoed past her coffin
on the way to our beds. The floorboards creaked,
the farmhouse moaned, buckling under the weight
of our footsteps and our grief.
After three days of mourning, we handed her body
over to the churchyard and its laws.

An Amish cemetery shuns flowers, photographs,
and other demonstrations of *worldliness*—
but what kind of mother leaves her children
to grieve without the simple comfort of color?
This was Grussy's wish: daffodils
strewn into her grave, integrated with the soil.
Each of us carried one, clutched between cold fingers.
All through the sermon, I stood beneath the canopy
cupping my hands around the bloom
as if it were a candle flame
in danger of being snuffed out.

When the ushers, preachers and elders left us alone
at the grave, we cast our flowers into the pit
and watched them bump against each other, disappearing
more with each shovel-full of dirt.

Although the stalks were cut off from their roots
and would not bloom again, it seemed we were
not burying, but planting.

II.

In Grussy's orchard, a misshapen tree:

> From one side, green apples ripen
> and drop. Summer blooms press
> against the Pennsylvania sky.

> The other side is stringy
> bark that never dries
> between rains.

> It crumples like wet paper
> in my hands —
> unwritten letters, unspoken
> love. The hapless side, the side that bears
> no fruit.

III.

In a hidden room, in another funeral
chamber lie the stoic remains
of my secret great-grandmother.
She is nameless, dark-skinned,

dressed in soft leather and beads.
Her thick black braids relax about her breast.
I have not seen her before.

Her skin feels leathery, an antelope hide,
not like the pillowy grandmothers I've known: plump
with hugs like rolling hills, voices as meek
and chirpy as barnyard sparrows.

I wonder whether this woman was more tender
alive. I imagine her voice as a summer wind
sweeping, unstoppable, across the Great Plains,
sending shivers through the grasses in her path.
I imagine her arms as sycamore boughs
holding up the sky —
her skin peeling, buckling under the weight
and sweat
of atmospheric pressure.

Balanced on her coffin, my fingertips itch
for one squeeze of her hand,
one twitch of her lip, one tremor
of her brow, one shared moment
between us: a meeting, a reunion,
a sign.

Instead, I tiptoe past the receiving line,
steal a covetous glance at my Indian cousins
and hope they will not discern me —
my tribal bones, the angles of my face.

Afterword
Contemporary Mennonite Poetry in North America

MENNONITE POETRY IN THE UNITED STATES

Contemporary Mennonite poetry began to emerge in the United States during the 1970s. Early poems by Warren Kliewer and Elmer Suderman, writers whose major genres became drama and fiction/memoir, were published in *Mennonite Life* and elsewhere. Dallas Wiebe, known for his fiction and memoirs as well as for his lengthy tenure as editor of the *Cincinnati Poetry Review*, also published a poetry chapbook and occasional poems. Yorifumi Yaguchi, a well-known Japanese poet who converted to Christianity through the work of Mennonite missionaries and who became a Mennonite minister himself, spent some time at Goshen College during the 1970s and published several chapbooks of poetry in English. Nick Lindsay, son of the poet Vachel Lindsay and a performance poet whose book of collected poems was recently published by Goshen's Pinchpenny Press, had a strong influence on Mennonite poetry in his role as poet in residence and visiting poet at Goshen College during the last three decades of the twentieth century. More than any other single poet, he began to convince large groups of Mennonites that poetry has a place in their midst; he mentored a significant number of the poets in this volume, including Jeff Gundy, Julia Kasdorf, Shari Wagner Miller, and Barbara Nickel.

The poets who first made an impact on important literary journals outside the Mennonite milieu, however, were several women who worked independently of each other and had no idea that they would someday lead off an anthology of poetry by writers of Mennonite origin. Jane Rohrer published eight poems in the *American Poetry Review* between 1977 and 1985 as well as in a number of other places. During approximately the same span of time, Anna Ruth Ediger Baehr and Jean Janzen began publishing their work in journals such as the *American Scholar* and *Poetry*. Baehr's "I Am Dancing with My Mennonite Father" was the first poem by a Mennonite writer on an overtly Mennonite topic to receive a major literary award: the Mary Elinore Smith Poetry Prize from the *American Scholar* in 1985.

When I first encountered this poem I thought Baehr must be a young M.F.A. graduate; only through researching poets for this anthology did I discover that she is, in fact, the oldest poet in this volume and that she first began publishing in literary journals after her retirement from elementary school teaching in 1978. While as a Mennonite writer it is encouraging to realize that one's tradition has given birth to poets, it is quite another to see the tradition itself — so little written about except in stereotype — taken seriously as the subject of art. My serendipitous discovery of Baehr's poem was exhilarating. Dancing was strictly forbidden by most Mennonites when I was growing up, although I had been allowed to go to high school dances, but the notion of dancing with one's father was unthinkable. One's father was the earthly model for one's heavenly father. Never before had a poem mirrored so closely my own Mennonite experience, with all of its complexity and contradictions, as did this lyric on the terrifying and tender prospect of a daughter who has learned how to dance tracing the steps with a father who has forbidden it. Not only did the poem reflect emotional geography familiar to many daughters of Mennonite fathers, it also showed me that a poem could bring together the two worlds I had polarized in my mind, that of Mennonite and that of poet. Apparently I was not the only Mennonite poet impressed by this work; the young Julia Spicher (to become Kasdorf) wrote to Baehr and asked permission to reprint "I Am Dancing with My Mennonite Father" in *Menno News*, the newsletter of the Manhattan Mennonite Fellowship, which she edited when she was a student at New York University. Baehr not only consented but mentioned Spicher as her newest Mennonite poet friend in a letter to her daughter, and Spicher sent Baehr some of her early work. Clearly these two award-winning poets had recognized each other across the generations through their work in print.

Throughout the 1980s small press and periodical publication among U.S. Mennonites continued to flourish. The 1990s saw an explosion of books by U.S. Mennonite poets published by university and small, independent presses. While Julia Kasdorf was the first to win a prestigious book publication award — the Agnes Lynch Starrett Poetry Prize — Juanita Brunk, Jeff Gundy, Jean Janzen, Keith Ratzlaff, and Betsy Sholl have published books with U.S. publishers during the 1990s, a number of them winning awards. Juanita Brunk won the Brittingham Prize, and Betsy Sholl won both the Associated Writing Program's Award Series in Poetry and the Felix Pollack Award. Jeff Gundy was short-listed for the Cleveland State Poetry Prize, and Jean Janzen was awarded a National Endowment for the Arts fellowship in 1995.

Jeff Gundy, whose first book, *Inquiries*, was published in 1992, the same year as Kasdorf's *Sleeping Preacher*, published poems throughout the 1980s in such well-known journals as the *Antioch Review*, *Ohio Review*, *Laurel Review*, and *Spoon River Quarterly*. While Gundy's poetic career in some ways parallels Kasdorf's, the subject matter of his poems is less recognizably Mennonite than is Kasdorf's in *Sleeping Preacher*. The ethnographic qualities of Kasdorf's Big Valley poems have attracted readers beyond the usual audience for contemporary poetry; Gundy's preoccupation with postmodernism has attracted a readership interested in philosophical and theological issues and experimental contemporary poetic form.

For the most part, contemporary Mennonite poets have sought book publishers beyond the Mennonite world, sensing either a lack of interest, editorial constraint, lack of literary prestige, or marketing strategies geared to the evangelical market as ill suited to their work. Good Books, on the other hand, a publishing firm in Intercourse, Pennsylvania, founded by Mennonites but not associated with the church, took a pioneering interest in Mennonite poetry when, in 1986, it brought out its first volume of poetry, *Three Mennonite Poets*, featuring work by poets from three different countries — Jean Janzen of California, Yorifumi Yaguchi of Japan, and David Waltner-Toews of Canada — suggesting the transnational aspect of Mennonite identity. Recently, Pandora Press, U.S., a small press affiliated with the Mennonite denomination, has taken an interest in publishing poetry and released two volumes by Mennonite poets in 2002 and 2003.

Good Books also published a magazine, *Festival Quarterly*, in the 1970s and 1980s, now defunct, that explored issues of Mennonites in the arts. Several other Mennonite periodicals, one from an academic source and two independent, have also supported the arts. *Mennonite Life*, published by Bethel College in North Newton, Kansas, has devoted one of its quarterly issues to the arts each year since 1989. It regularly publishes interviews with and poetry by Mennonite poets and is available online at www.bethelks.edu/mennonitelife. *Mennonot: A Journal for Mennos on the Margins*, an independent zine edited by Sheri Hostetler focusing on humor, parody, cultural critique, and the arts, has repeatedly published poetry by writers of Mennonite origin. *Kairos: Arts and Letters of the Mennonite Church*, founded in 1997 as an outgrowth of the Cincinnati Mennonite Arts Weekend, has offered an outlet for U.S. Mennonite writers and artists. In addition, Dallas Wiebe, editor of the *Cincinnati Poetry Review*, became aware of other Mennonite poets in his capacity as editor and published some of their work.

U.S. poets Janet Kauffman, Betsy Sholl, and Juanita Brunk illustrate the ways in which the term "Mennonite" transcends strict cultural or religious definitions in this anthology. Kauffman's father was raised in a Mennonite family, and Kauffman spent a great deal of time with her paternal grandparents as she was growing up. Her experience with Mennonites is steeped in the experience of an agricultural lifestyle in which people work interdependently with each other and the land. While today she is known primarily for her experimental fiction, Kauffman's two volumes of poetry, one of them an Associated Writing Program award winner, express an affinity for work and the land that has been part of Mennonite life for centuries.

Brunk, raised in a Mennonite family, does not consider herself Mennonite today. Her poetry in *Brief Landing on the Earth's Surface* finds redemption in moments of being and presence, the miraculous in the ordinary. Sholl's experience with Mennonites has been as an adult. For five years her husband pastored a Mennonite church in Maine, and she has attended Mennonite Fellowships in Pittsburgh and Lewistown, Pennsylvania, finding a kinship through community and worship rather than through ancestral family ties or upbringing. Todd Davis and David Wright became Mennonites as adults, choosing the faith as one compatible with their own spiritual values. Both Davis and Wright celebrate family and connection in their work, reaching out to the world and the people around them; Wright does so in a city landscape, Davis in the context of the natural world. All of these poets embrace the world in a sort of sensory transcendentalism, celebrating the spiritual in the sensual and ordinary textures of earthly life.

Of U.S. Mennonite poets writing today, Jeff Gundy is the most interested in theological questions, although he explores them, as do the above poets, through the ordinary everyday world. This dialectic between the divine presence and the details of daily living reflects most accurately the tension in the Mennonite community where hard work, order, and attention to detail are valued but not viewed as manifestations of the divine as they were, for instance, in the austere aesthetics of the Shaker community. Keith Ratzlaff, a poet and scholar who grew up in a conservative, rural Mennonite community in Nebraska, combines pop culture and the visual arts with his concern for the body's vulnerability and his love of nature in his elegiac poetry. His award-winning book, *Man under a Pear Tree*, was inspired by the paintings of Paul Klee when Ratzlaff was living in London for several years and was searching for a new idiom. David Wright, a poet and teacher as well as a scholar who writes about Gundy's poetry, recently joined the Mennonite Church. His work reflects the spirit of the Mennonite community, infused with the energetic vision of a newcomer.

Raylene Hinz-Penner, Julia Kasdorf, Ann Hostetler, and Shari Miller Wagner explore a variety of perspectives on relationships, the construction of memory, the identity of the artist, and the legacy of ancestral voices, especially those of women. Hinz-Penner, a western Mennonite from the General Conference group, writes poetry with a bold, fresh voice that honors the individual perspective and imagination through her poems to Georgia O'Keeffe. Kasdorf's poetry reveals the degree to which Mennonite identity is imbued with the stories of community, as well as the struggle of a woman in that society to achieve possession of her own body and voice. Wagner's poetry portrays the Mennonite community as enacted in such rituals as playing Rook and spontaneous hymn singing, while Hostetler's seeks to trace the survival of artistic impulse throughout the generations. Barbara Nickel, Carmen Horst, and Jessica Smucker Falcón represent a younger generation of writers who have benefited from reading and studying with Mennonite and other poets. Their compression of imagery and ironic reference to Mennonite touchstones of identity illustrate how the experience of Mennonite culture is transmitted and reformed.

As interest in poetry and other forms of imaginative writing among U.S. Mennonite readers has surged during the past decade, poetry has become, in addition to literary expression, a discourse through which writers of Mennonite background can describe and explore connections between their heritage and the multiple frames of reference they inhabit in a postmodern society. The poetry itself, as Hildi Froese Tiessen has recently argued, has the potential to dismantle monolithic constructs of Mennonite identity by providing rich and varied images, from multiple poetic perspectives, of what it means to be a member of the Mennonite community as well as to engage with other communities of language.

One theme that connects many of the poets in this anthology is the desire to articulate various worlds of experience — bringing them into dialogue, or even collision, with one another. A surprising number of the poets in this volume have grown up in cross-cultural contexts, traveled extensively, or otherwise negotiated multiple worlds. Poetry becomes one place in which fragments of these experiences are connected. Some of the poets focus on the shifting contexts of community across generations. Others focus on the juxtaposition of oral folk communities with communities of writing and literature. Some center on place, land, the created world. Still others explore the problems of knowledge and faith in a postmodern context. Together their work charts a geography of concern that honors individual experience and voice in conversation with diverse constructions of community and world.

MENNONITE POETRY IN CANADA

During my research on U.S. Mennonite poets, I became aware of an established Mennonite literary arts community in Canada centered in Winnipeg, Manitoba. It emerged in the 1960s and 1970s, then developed rapidly during the 1980s, when the Canadian government offered publishing grants to ethnic writers, and it continues to flourish. While Canadian literary culture, Canadian Mennonite history, and Canadian Mennonite immigration patterns differ in significant ways from their counterparts in the United States, the work of Canadian poets of Mennonite origin has been influential, encouraging, and in some ways critical for the more recently emerging U.S. Mennonite poets. But because of the structures governing publication and book circulation within and between the two countries, few of these poets' books have been readily available to U.S. readers. I have included in this volume a selection from major Canadian writers in order to represent the full range of North American poetry by writers of Mennonite origin. In the case of this anthology, religious, ethnic, and linguistic criteria cross national boundaries.

All Mennonite writers since the mid 1960s owe a debt to Canadian novelist Rudy Wiebe, whose first novel, *Peace Shall Destroy Many*, both created a sensation (not entirely positive) among Mennonites and marked the start of a distinguished literary career. From the beginning, connections between writers in the United States and Canada have been important, and many of the poets have roots in both countries, but the contemporary literary scenes in each nation have also developed independently.

Wiebe's *Peace Shall Destroy Many* is an ambitious novel, problematizing within the context of a Canadian Russian Mennonite community the central Mennonite teaching of nonresistance and criticizing the closed nature of the church community. Wiebe's portrait of the Mennonite patriarchal community was bound to draw criticism from the community itself, and he was severely criticized by his Mennonite Brethren denomination to the point of feeling compelled to resign his editorship of *Mennonite Mirror* — a situation that dramatizes one version of the narrative of tension between the Mennonite community and its artists. Nonetheless, Wiebe has continued to speak eloquently outside of the community as a novelist, winning the Governor General's Award for Fiction twice in his career — an unprecedented honor — and maintains ties with a Mennonite Brethren church community, where he is also a lay minister, suggesting an eventual rapprochement between the artist and the community.

Any novelist or poet from within the community taking the community as a subject must see Wiebe's earlier experience as a caveat. Lyric poetry, however, compared to the novel, is a fluid genre with the capacity for representing social constructions of reality and social relations without fixing their relationships to one another. For the aspiring Mennonite writer who wishes to create some authorial distance, lyric poetry also has the advantage of being far more inconspicuous both in its production and in its consumption than a novel. It is possible to publish poems in literary journals for decades without attracting much notice. Thus many of the poets in this anthology began writing poetry out of some sort of personal calling or interior conversation rather than in overt dialogue with a community. Many have pursued poetry writing in connection with another profession, most commonly teaching. A number of the poems explore complex and even taboo areas of Mennonite culture but have done so without attracting much criticism from the Mennonite community because no one from the community was paying much attention — that is, the poetry was published in literary journals. On the other hand, Mennonites in North America have changed enormously over the forty years since Wiebe's novel was first published, becoming consumers of most forms of cultural production — literature, television, film, web technology — from the broader society. Mennonite higher education has flourished over the last century, inevitably shaping the consciousness of the church and the culture as well. The development of literature by writers of Mennonite origin, along with a slow but increasing audience for their work among Mennonite and other readers, seems a logical outgrowth of this situation.

Working with the poems of writers from two different regions of cultural production has led to many perplexing questions about Mennonites, as well as about ethnicity and national literatures. First, I had to decide whether "Mennonite" was solely a religious affiliation or a distinctive cultural and ethnic heritage that shared common features with other North American immigrant subcultures. Could a generations-old immigrant religious group that had retained its distinct identity over four centuries, always resisting amalgamation into Protestantism, be considered an ethnic group? Did the emergence of recent achievement in the literary and visual arts signify a new stage in the group's cultural assimilation into the mainstream of Anglo-European artistic heritage?

The popular use of the term "ethnicity" in the United States as a euphemism for race differs from the Canadian use of the term to designate cultural features. In Canada, Mennonites are considered to be a leading group of ethnic writers, with a vigorous, active cultural center in Winnipeg, Manitoba. Hildi Froese Tiessen writes in her introduction to a collection of Mennonite literature in the *New Quarterly*, "Among the minority-culture literary communities in Canada, few, it could be argued, are at present more productive — or more visible as a literary community — than Mennonites." She goes on to emphasize that these writers are "by no means individually alien or alienated from the literary 'mainstream' (where many of them have found a secure enough place)." In the early 1990s the leading literary journals the *New Quarterly* and *Prairie Fire* published issues devoted to Mennonite writers and writing.

It is significant that the writing of Di Brandt, Patrick Friesen, Sarah Klassen, and Audrey Poetker was nurtured in relation to a vital contemporary Mennonite arts community in Winnipeg, in which "Mennonite" is often considered a cultural rather than a religious designation. No such geographical or discursive community exists for U.S. Mennonite poets at present. In 1997 a new literary journal, *Rhubarb*, edited by Victor Jerrett

Enns, emerged from the Canadian Mennonite literary community. It is publishing work by both U.S. and Canadian poets. In 2002 twenty-four poets and fiction writers — twelve from each country — were featured as invited plenary readers at "Mennonite/s Writing: An International Conference," cosponsored by Goshen College and by Conrad Grebel University College at the University of Waterloo, Ontario, and hosted at Goshen. Perhaps the future of a literary community among North American Mennonite readers lies in greater communication between geographically separated communities of poets.

In the early work of Di Brandt and Patrick Friesen, both prolific and well-known Canadian poets born into conservative rural Manitoba Mennonite communities, the portrayal of community is much harsher than in Kasdorf's *Sleeping Preacher*, though similar concerns with language, imagination, gender, autonomy, and freedom of expression surface. Although these poets long for communion with their readers, their work variously reflects the painful price of community: experiences of physical pain, lack of communication, suffocating silence, unarticulated rage. Friesen's *The Shunning* deals with the departure from community as rupture. Brandt frames communities of women within existing patriarchal structures, especially those between mothers and daughters. Her work openly confronts abuses too often protected by silence in the community. The work of Jean Janzen, a Mennonite Brethren poet of Canadian origin who has lived most of her adult life in California, suggests both the price of community in the Old World — addressing such subjects as the suicide of her maternal grandmother — and the potential for communication between generations in the new. David Waltner-Toews, on the other hand, takes a different approach, emphasizing family connection and bridging different frames of reference through the skillful use of story, dialect, and humor in his poetry, especially in his Tante Tina poems. His concern with ecology and the global community, an outgrowth of his Mennonite beliefs in peace, justice, and sharing of resources, is voiced in his poetry. While Brandt and Friesen have strong roots in ethnic Mennonite communities, neither of them is associated with a Mennonite congregation today. On the other hand, Waltner-Toews has maintained connections with his community of origin, and Janzen has been and continues to be vitally involved with a Mennonite Brethren congregation in Fresno, California, since its founding in the 1960s, as well as with Mennonite education in her teaching at Eastern Mennonite University and Fresno Pacific University. She has also authored hymns inspired by the medieval female mystics Juliann of Norwich, ten of which appear in the most recent hymnal of the Mennonite Church.

Several Canadian poets address the history of Mennonite identity in martyrdom and communities of exile. These are primarily poets from the Russian Mennonite tradition, whose experience of persecution and migration is much more recent than that of Swiss Mennonites. They have a stronger connection to an arts tradition within their Russian Mennonite heritage, which also embraced the use of musical instruments, primarily the piano, in worship services. Sarah Klassen and Jean Janzen are two such poets, both of whom have made extensive visits to Europe and to the sites of early persecution. Barbara Nickel's first book, *The Gladys Elegies*, is centered in her practice as a classical violinist as much as it is in the stories of her Russian Mennonite heritage. Common themes among these poets include community, memory, anger, loss, and the complex and often uncertain project of creating an identity out of multiple voices and fragments as an artist of faith in a postmodern world. All three are also actively involved in the practice or appreciation of visual and/or musical arts.

MENNONITE VOICES, COMMUNITIES, AND HETEROGENEITY
While Mennonites are an Anabaptist Christian denomination that formed during the Reformation, they also have the characteristics of an ethnic subculture, intensified by a community ethic, genealogy, and specific history. The vital Mennonite community, committed and dedicated to the congregational unit, maintains mutually accountable relationships within that community. Each church takes on its distinct dynamic in its embodied practice of faith — thus the incredible diversity among practicing Mennonites today and among the origins of the Mennonite poets in this volume: from Kleine Gemeinde and Amish to Evangelical Mennonite Brethren and General Conference Mennonite, from the "Old" Mennonite Church to recent converts to newly founded urban congregations. The fastest-growing segment of the Mennonite Church worldwide, currently in Africa and Latin America, with a growing presence in the Middle East and Indonesia, is far more concerned with the alleviation of suffering caused by economic and political injustice than with the finer points of faith and practice that often consume Mennonites of European descent. Such diversity is almost impossible to represent symbolically, but to create an anthology of poets of "Mennonite origins" is inevitably to engage in the identity discussion.

Today there are approximately 416,000 Mennonites in North America. Recent Mennonite congregations in Africa, South America, India, and the Far East more than double that number to a total of a million Mennonite Church members worldwide. Most Mennonites are pacifists who believe that the law of God takes precedence over the law of the nation, although they live in harmony with the nation when their religious beliefs are not called into question. They identify themselves as followers of Jesus Christ who take the text of the Sermon on the Mount as central to their understanding of the Bible. They believe that Christ calls Christians to express God's love to each other through their community and congregational life and to all of humanity by helping to meet the physical as well as the spiritual needs of others. While some of the poets in this anthology are active participants in the Mennonite community, others have found the actual, human experience of lived Christian community to be flawed, suffocating, and even harmful. The anthology embraces all of these perspectives as valuable in understanding a large, complex picture of the possibilities of artistic representation and experimentation in the repertoire of poets who have been shaped by Mennonite faith and community.

THE TROUBLED BIRTH OF
THE ARTIST IN MENNONITE CULTURE

Through informal interviews with a number of literary and visual artists from the past several generations of Mennonites, I have gathered stories of a painful, injurious struggle as part of the history of the emergence of a poetic voice from the Mennonite community — a struggle damaging mostly for the artist but for the community as well. In an ethnic faith where God's calling for one's life is not necessarily perceived as being aligned to one's talents, gifts, or joys, the creative gifts that propelled artists to expression also forced them out of communities where there was little tolerance and even less acceptance of their work. In many cases where the community tolerated the artist's work, it did not invite or embrace the imaginative productions of its creative members unless they were expressed through such channels as didactic children's literature or illustration. Thus the community did not nurture or value the artists who emerged within it. Rather, artists — as is the case with many ethnic subcultures — were viewed with suspicion or even hostility. Some Mennonite communities have been more hospitable to the arts than others. Those who welcome artists tend to have already incorporated a complex dialogue with the arts into their theology, borrowing elements of liturgy and music and dance from other contexts in their worship services. But most Mennonite communities have protected their traditions by defending themselves against assimilation into other groups, forming invisible but rigid boundaries about acceptable behaviors and beliefs for their members. Mennonite artists emerging from such traditional communities have often been motivated by anger at perceived injustice or hypocrisy to leave the community, either becoming vociferous critics or disconnecting themselves entirely. In recent years, some of these artists have begun to return to or at least to create a linguistic suspension bridge between their artistic and ethnic identities.

Mennonite suspicion of the arts is rooted in a literal interpretation of scripture that raises a number of questions. Does a disciple of Christ have time for art? Doesn't art elevate individuals at the expense of the group? And doesn't art (figurative language and metaphor included) lead us away from truth rather than toward it? These questions and others are answered beautifully in a children's novel by Elaine Sommers Rich entitled *Hannah Elizabeth*, published by Harper and Row after a Mennonite publisher had rejected it. Hannah, a child with a poetic spirit and love of imaginative literature taken to task for reading poetry and fiction by the literalist members of her congregation, is vindicated by her benevolent bishop, who reads to his congregation figurative passages from the Bible. *Hannah Elizabeth*, given to me by my parents, was an important book in my childhood, for it showed that some Mennonites cared about literature and could create a representation of the artist's quest that I could place on my bookshelf next to works by such favorites as Marguerite D'Angeli, Lois Lenski, and Louisa May Alcott. It also showed me that Mennonite subjects — in fiction — could be interesting to non-Mennonite publishers.

Most attempts to describe the Mennonite experience in narrative appear to embody something of the assimilation-friendly paradigm of American literature expressed in Thomas Wolfe's words: "You can't go home again." It would seem that, regrettably, the only possibility for protagonists of such narratives was to leave behind their communities, either out of anger, rebellion, conviction, or a desire for greater understanding or self-expression. Such a paradigm is based on linear models of development and progress as being simultaneous with alienation and individuation. The individual, born into a restrictive community, must emerge from the strictures of loyalty to that community in order to embrace the open horizons of democracy and the American dream — albeit that freedom is sometimes portrayed as hazardous, empty, and terrifying. The paradigm is also based, however, on a modernist model of identity that assumes an individual has one developing self rather than a myriad of selves developed in interaction with other selves and communities.

Pathbreaking work on Mennonites in literature was done by scholar and anthologist Hildi Froese Tiessen (in Canada), who collected the work of Canadian Mennonite poets and fiction writers in special issues of the *New Quarterly* and *Prairie Fire* in the early 1990s and who edited an anthology of short fiction, *Liars and Rascals*. Before Tiessen's work, only one Mennonite had attempted to address questions of the role of literature in Mennonite culture: John Ruth — a historian, autobiographer, and Ph.D. in English who is also a Mennonite minister — in *Mennonite Identity and Literary Art*. In 1993 Al Reimer — a literary critic and novelist — attempted to theorize the origins of Mennonite literature, focusing on the Russian Mennonite experience, in *Mennonite Literary Voices*. (Both studies are out of print.) According to Ruth, the proper role of the Mennonite artist is to use the materials — such as stories — provided by the community to make art that is of use to the community. Yet Ruth's exhortation to Mennonites to create a Mennonite art is peppered with quotes from such worldly writers as Tolstoy and Tillich, whom he studied at Harvard. Reimer's more recent criticism on the Canadian Mennonite literary tradition focuses on the conflict of individuals seeking to separate from the community. In 1996 the *Mennonite Quarterly Review* (*MQR*) published the first survey of contemporary Mennonite poetry by Jeff Gundy. In a subsequent issue on postmodernism, a number of Mennonite scholars and artists attempted to interrogate and revise traditional models of community. In 1998 *MQR* published a landmark issue — the first of its kind — "Mennonite/s Writing in the U.S." It appears as though older paradigms of literary productivity and piety are beginning to give way to new models as literary discourse gains strength and credibility among Mennonites.

Recent theories of postmodernism, which posit the self as a construct and identity as the intersection of self and world on a complicated map that includes circles and switchbacks as well as broad linear highways, enable us to view artistic and literary production as a site at which multiple cultural identities overlap. These postmodern models correct earlier modernist models of community that posit hegemonic identities for communities that are centrist and rigid — one is either inside or outside. In such modernist configurations of community, poets were marginalized and had to leave in order to find their voices.

Postmodernism has also drawn increasing attention to the patchwork nature of culture. For instance, in her discussion of Faith Ringgold's Paris series quilts in *Racechanges*, Susan Gubar demonstrates that the interaction of traditions and artistic or literary forms is extremely complex. By combining the quilting of her African American heritage and the French Impressionism of her education in Western culture, along with the influences of the cultured and talented women (and men) in her family, Ringgold has created works of art that question the relationship of different cultural images to one another. Borrowing, too, has always characterized Mennonite culture. The a cappella four-part harmony that has for generations been the beloved cultural legacy of Mennonite worship services was actually borrowed from the nineteenth-century singing-school and Sunday school traditions and was incorporated into Mennonite worship services only in the early twentieth century. The Old Order Amish, who eschewed Sunday school as an unnecessary compartmentalization of their community, still sing in unison.

Theories of narrative stemming from American Indian literature have been especially helpful to me in critiquing the modernist model of the autonomous and singular individual developing over time — which makes the Mennonite artist flourishing within a Mennonite community a seeming impossibility — and in reframing the movement of the individual away from the group and toward an immersion in other images and possibilities. William Bevis, in his essay about American Indian literature, "Coming Home," posits the cyclical return of the individual to the community as part of the plot of American Indian writing. The poets in this anthology engage in a kind of "coming home" — not to outmoded notions of community but to an imaginative reinscription of Mennonite community that embraces the voices of outsiders and heretics as well as those who are centered in Mennonite practice, substituting a community of imagination and voice for the literal communities in which many of the poets were born and raised.

That poetry is now written and read by Mennonites and has an audience within both the literary and Mennonite communities testifies to the U.S. cultural interest in multiethnic stories and traditions and to a new openness to poetic forms among literate Mennonites. Both conditions are necessary to the production and publication of this work: the larger culture's acknowledgment that a complex and specific history is the heritage of all Americans — whether they are aware of this fact or not — and the Mennonite community's acknowledgment and valuing of the kinds of challenges and questions that artistic exploration and representation pose.

Further Reading

Beck, Ervin. "Mennonite/s Writing in Canada." http://www.goshen.edu/
~ervinb/bibliographies/can-biblio.html.

———. "Mennonite/s Writing in the U.S." http://www.goshen.edu/~ervinb/
bibliographies/menno_us_bib/BeckBib.html.

Beck, Ervin, and John D. Roth, eds. "Mennonite/s Writing in the U.S." *Mennonite
Quarterly Review* 72 (Oct. 1998).

———. Special issue. "Mennonite/s Writing: An International Conference."
Mennonite Quarterly Review 92 (Oct. 2003).

Brandt, Di. *Dancing Naked: Narrative Strategies for Writing across Centuries*. Toronto:
Mercury Press, 1997.

Gundy, Jeff. "American Mennonite Poetry and Poets: Beyond Dr. Johnson's Dog."
Mennonite Quarterly Review 1 (Jan. 1997): 5–41.

Hostetler, Beulah. *American Mennonites and Protestant Movements: A Community
Paradigm*. Studies in Mennonite and Anabaptist History No. 28. Scottdale, Pa.:
Herald Press, 1987. Reprint, Eugene, Or.: Wipf and Stock, 2002.

Hutcheon, Linda. "Four Views on Ethnicity." *PMLA* 113 (Jan. 1, 1998), 28–33.

Kasdorf, Julia. *The Body and the Book: Writing from a Mennonite Life*. Baltimore:
Johns Hopkins University Press, 2001.

Reimer, Al. *Mennonite Literary Voices: Past and Present*. North Newton, Kans.:
Bethel College, 1993.

Roth, John D., and Ervin Beck, eds. *Migrant Muses: Mennonites Writing in the U.S.*
Goshen, Ind.: Mennonite Historical Society, 1998.

Ruth, John. *Mennonite Identity and Literary Art*. Scottdale, Pa.: Herald Press, 1978.

Tiessen, Hildi Froese, ed. "Mennonite/s Writing in Canada." *New Quarterly* 10,
nos. 1/2 (spring/summer 1990).

———. "New Mennonite Writing." *Prairie Fire* 11, no. 2 (summer 1990).

Permissions

Anna Ruth Ediger Baehr: "I Am Dancing with My Mennonite Father" (originally published in the *American Scholar*), "Cleaning the Cistern," "Ritual," and "I Will Not Pretend" from *Moonflowers at Dusk* (Birnham Wood Graphics, 1996). Copyright 1996 by Anna Ruth Ediger Baehr. Reprinted by permission of Beth Bullard. "Christina" copyright 1998 by Beth Bullard and appears by her permission.

Di Brandt: "when i was five i thought heaven was located" and "my mother found herself one late summer" from *questions i asked my mother* (Turnstone Press, 1997). Copyright 1997 by Di Brandt. Reprinted by permission of Turnstone Press. "nonresistance, or love Mennonite style" from *Agnes in the Sky* (Turnstone Press, 1990). Copyright 1990 by Di Brandt. Reprinted by permission of Turnstone Press. "there are no words for me in Gaza, for what i saw" from *Jerusalem Beloved* (Turnstone Press, 1995). Copyright 1995 by Di Brandt. Reprinted by permission of the author and Turnstone Press. "the great dark rush of mothering" and "little one, black angel" from *mother, not mother* (Mercury Press, 1996). Reprinted by permission of the author.

Juanita Brunk: "My Father's Tongue," "All Sweet Things, Like Forgiveness, Are a Falling" (both originally published in *Poet Lore*), "On This Earth" (originally published in *Passages North*), "Letter to Myself as a Child," "Where My Mother Cries," and "Papaya: Lancaster County" from *Brief Landing on the Earth's Surface* (University of Wisconsin Press, 1996). Copyright 1996 by the Board of Regents of the University of Wisconsin System. Reprinted by permission of the publisher.

Todd Davis: "Elkhart, Indiana" (originally published in *Aethlon: The Journal of Sport Literature*), "Building Walls" (originally published in *Yankee*), "Ripe," "Love Letter to My Mother, Sixteen Years after the Fact," and "Loving the Flesh" from *Ripe* (Bottom Dog Press, 2002). Copyright 2002 by Todd Davis. Reprinted by permission of the author.

Jessica Smucker Falcón: "Burial Clothes" originally published in the *Hawai'i Review*. "Indian Locks" originally published in the *Spoon River Poetry Review*. An earlier version of "Hemispheres" appeared in *Inside Magazine*, Lancaster, Pennsylvania. All poems copyright by Jessica Smucker Falcón. Reprinted by permission of the author.

Patrick Friesen: "clearing poems" from *The Breath You Take from the Lord* (Harbour Publishing, 2002). Copyright 2002 by Patrick Friesen. Reprinted by permission of Patrick Friesen and Harbour Publishing. "pa poem 1: firstborn" and "pa poem 4: naked and nailed" from *Unearthly Horses* (Turnstone Press, 1984). Copyright 1984 by Patrick Friesen. Reprinted by permission of Turnstone Press. "the moon in the streets" from *Saint Mary at Main* (J. Gordon Shillingford, 1998). Copyright 1998 by Patrick Friesen. Reprinted with permission of the Muses' Company.

Jeff Gundy: "The Cookie Poem" and "Old Water" (originally published in *Kairos*) from *Rhapsody with Dark Matter* (Bottom Dog Press, 2000). Copyright 2000 by

Hilberry, and James Tipton [Wayne State University Press, 1976]) from *The Weather Book* (Texas Tech Press, 1981). Copyright 1981 by Janet Kauffman. All poems reprinted by permission of the author.

Sarah Klassen: "Making the Rate" from *Simone Weil: Songs of Hunger and Love* (Wolsak and Wynn, 1999). Copyright 1999 by Sarah Klassen. Reprinted by permission of the publisher. "Act of Mercy" from *Violence and Mercy* (Netherlandic Press, 1991). Copyright 1991 by Sarah Klassen. Reprinted by permission of the author. "Russian Fables" from *Borderwatch* (Netherlandic Press, 1993). Copyright 1993 by Sarah Klassen. Reprinted by permission of the author. "Artist and Medium" and "Repenting" from *Dangerous Elements* (Quarry Press, 1998). Copyright 1998 by Sarah Klassen. Reprinted by permission of author.

Leonard Neufeldt: "Yarrow," "The man with the glass eye," and "The tree with the hole in our front yard" from *Yarrow* (Black Moss Press, 1993). Copyright 1993 by Leonard Neufeldt. "Dyke View Berry Farm" from *Raspberrying* (Black Moss Press, 1991). Copyright 1991 by Leonard Neufeldt. All poems reprinted by permission of the author.

Barbara Nickel: "Lines" and "Three Poems for Violin" from *The Gladys Elegies* (Coteau Books, 1997). Copyright 1997 by Barbara Nickel. Reprinted by permission of the publisher.

Audrey Poetker: "she tries to tell him" from *standing all through the night* (Turnstone Press, 1992). Copyright 1992 by Audrey Poetker-Thiessen. Reprinted by permission of Turnstone Press. "Symbols of Fertility," "Fallen women," and "My kingdom is of this world" from *Making Strange to Yourself* (Turnstone Press, 1999). Copyright 1999 by Turnstone Press. Reprinted by permission of Turnstone Press.

Keith Ratzlaff: "Necessity" from *New Winter Light* (Loess Hills Press, 1994). Copyright 1994 by Keith Ratzlaff. Reprinted by permission of the author. "Rough-Cut Head" (originally published in the *Threepenny Review*), "Gospel," "Group Portrait with Ukuleles," and "My Students against the Cemetery Pines" (all originally published in *Poetry Northwest*) from *Man under a Pear Tree* (Anhinga Press, 1997). Copyright 1997 by Keith Ratzlaff. Reprinted by permission of Anhinga Press. "Dill" originally published in the *North American Review* 287, no. 1 (Jan.–Feb. 2002). Reprinted by permission of the author.

Jane Rohrer: "In the Kitchen before Dinner," "Mennonite Funeral in the Shenandoah Valley," "The Gearshift Poem," "Room 703," "Hotel," and "Stopping by Fields on a Snowy Afternoon" originally published in the *American Poetry Review*. Copyright by Jane Rohrer. Reprinted by permission of the author.

Betsy Sholl: "Autobiography in Third Person" (originally published in the *Cimarron Review*), "Don't Explain" (originally published in the *Indiana Review*), and "Redbud" (originally published in *Field*) from *Don't Explain* (University of Wisconsin Press, 1997). Copyright 1997 by the Board of Regents of the University of Wisconsin System. Reprinted by permission of the publisher. "Soup Kitchen" from *The Red Line* (University of Pittsburgh Press, 1992). Copyright 1992 by Betsy Sholl. Reprinted by permission of the University of Pittsburgh Press. "Late

Index